Bold Women
in Texas History

Don Blevins

Bold Women
in Texas History

Don Blevins

2012
Mountain Press Publishing Company
Missoula, Montana

Library of Congress Cataloging-in-Publication Data

Blevins, Don, 1933-
 Bold women in Texas history / Donald Blevins.
     p. cm.
 Includes bibliographical references and index.
 ISBN 978-0-87842-583-9 (pbk. : alk. paper)
 1. Women—Texas—Biography. 2. Women—Texas—History.
 3. Texas—Biography. I. Title.
 CT3260.B613 2012
 920.7209764—dc23
                          2011029461

PRINTED IN THE U.S.A.

MP Mountain Press
PUBLISHING COMPANY
P.O. Box 2399 • Missoula, MT 59806 • 406-728-1900
800-234-5308 • info@mtnpress.com
www.mountain-press.com

To my family

Contents

Acknowledgments

Any historical writing must, of necessity, be backed by many sources. This book is no different. Special thanks go to the Daughters of the Republic of Texas, the staff at the Alamo, and especially Martha Utterback. John Anderson of the Texas State Library and Archives Commission was a great source. My gratitude also to Newton Warzecha, Presidio La Bahia, Goliad; the staff at Austin History Center, Austin Public Library; and Suzanne Pate, Babe Didrikson Zaharias Foundation.

This book could not have been completed without the excellent guidance of Gwen McKenna, my editor at Mountain Press. Her knowledge, assistance, and direction were most important.

There are others to whom I am indebted for their help in preparing this book. My apologies to anyone I have overlooked by name.

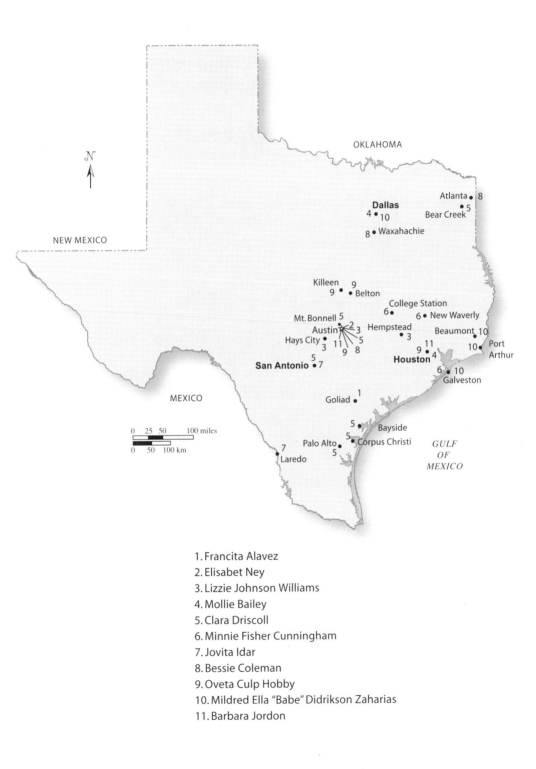

OKLAHOMA

NEW MEXICO

MEXICO

Atlanta • 8

Dallas
4 • 10   Bear Creek • 5

8 • Waxahachie

Killeen   9
9 • • Belton

College Station
Mt. Bonnell 5   6 •   6 • New Waverly
2 • 3 Hempstead   Beaumont • 10
Austin ✳ 3   10 • Port
Hays City • • 5   Arthur
3 11 9 8   9 11
San Antonio 5   Houston 4
• 7   6 • • 10
Galveston

1
Goliad •

5 • Bayside
Palo Alto 5 • • Corpus Christi   *GULF*
7 5   *OF*
Laredo   *MEXICO*

0 25 50   100 miles
0   50   100 km

1. Francita Alavez
2. Elisabet Ney
3. Lizzie Johnson Williams
4. Mollie Bailey
5. Clara Driscoll
6. Minnie Fisher Cunningham
7. Jovita Idar
8. Bessie Coleman
9. Oveta Culp Hobby
10. Mildred Ella "Babe" Didrikson Zaharias
11. Barbara Jordon

Introduction

Within the pages of this book are brief biographies of eleven Texas women who left an indelible mark not only on the Lone Star State, but on the nation as well. Among these trailblazers, champions, and heroines are pioneering Hispanic journalist Jovita Idar; sculptor Elisabet Ney; cattle baroness Lizzie Johnson Williams; philanthropist Clara Driscoll; progressive activist Minnie Fisher Cunningham; and others who are described below.

Our first story looks at a young Mexican girl, still in her teens, who defied her countrymen to help wounded and mistreated Anglo-American prisoners during the Texas Revolution. Because of her actions, Texans called her "the Angel of Goliad." We also learn about two women of African American descent who fought long, hard battles against racism, sexism, and prejudice to break down— or at least punch holes in—the barriers of their time. The ambitious and tenacious Bessie Coleman became the first black woman in the United States to be awarded a pilot's license, which she had to obtain in France because no American flight school would accept a woman. A generation later came the equally intrepid Barbara Jordan. Unable to enroll in the then-segregated University of Texas, Barbara attended the predominantly black Texas Southern University, then law school at Boston University. In 1972 she became the first black woman elected to national office from a Southern state. After an outstanding record in Congress, she became a tenured professor at the University of Texas, the same school from which she had been barred twenty-seven years before. Some said she spoke with "the voice of God."

Another fascinating figure is Mollie Kirkland, who at age fourteen, against the wishes of her parents, eloped with circus performer Gus Bailey. The young couple formed a traveling theatrical troupe that would delight hundreds of thousands of rural residents over the years. During the Civil War, Mollie served as a nurse and, on several occasions, as a spy. Returning to show business after the war, the Bailey family expanded their enterprise, which eventually became the legendary spectacle of early-1900s Texas known as Aunt Mollie's Circus.

Mildred Didrikson, a born tomboy from a humble background, grew up to be the mid-twentieth-century sports phenomenon known as "Babe" Didrikson Zaharias. As a youngster, Babe could beat her schoolmates in virtually any athletic endeavor. She picked up her nickname during a game of sandlot baseball in which she was compared to Babe Ruth. An all-around athlete, she entered the only professional sport truly open to women of her time: golf. Taking the golf world by storm, Babe won every women's golf title in existence during the 1940s, and she was named the Woman Athlete of the Half-Century in 1950. Struck with cancer in 1953, Babe was told she would never play tournament golf again. Only a few months after undergoing surgery, however, she was back on the circuit and won five more tournaments before her untimely death in 1956.

Perhaps no other female Texan has received more honors, awards, and accolades than Oveta Culp Hobby. At the young age of twenty, Oveta was appointed legislative parliamentarian, a position she held for six years. In 1931 she married newspaper publisher and former governor William Pettus Hobby, with whom she worked on the *Houston Post-Dispatch*. When World War II broke out, the Pentagon asked Oveta to organize a women's auxiliary for the army. Originally known as the WAAC (Women's Army Auxiliary Corps), the unit later became the WAC (Women's Army Corps), part of the regular army. In the 1950s, President Dwight Eisenhower appointed Oveta director of a newly formed federal agency called the Department of Health, Education, and Welfare, making her the second woman ever to hold a Cabinet-level position. It was in this job that Oveta made a bold decision to dispense the largely untested Salk polio vaccine, the drug that within a decade virtually eradicated the dreaded disease.

These eleven biographies provide but a sampling of the scores of Lone Star daughters who not only held their own, but changed history. The state of Texas could not be more proud.

Statue of Francita Alavez at Presidio La Bahía, near Goliad —Courtesy Presidio La Bahía, Goliad, Texas

1

Francita Alavez

"ANGEL OF GOLIAD"

On March 6, 1836, several thousand
Mexican troops broke through the crumbling
walls of the Alamo Mission in San Antonio, taking the lives of some 189 Tejanos (Texas Mexicans) and Anglos
(white Americans). Those Texians (American residents of the territory that is now the state of Texas) who gave their lives defending
this indefensible structure had expected reinforcements that never
arrived. When the Mexicans attacked, they were trapped inside
the mission and badly outnumbered. Nevertheless, they chose to
stand their ground, even in the face of annihilation.

The Battle of the Alamo has been glorified in songs, books, mov-
ies, and other media, and rightly so, yet the Texians' defeat here
was meaningful more as a symbol than as a military loss. After the
slaughter, "Remember the Alamo" became a rallying cry for fighting Texians. A month and a half after the Texians met defeat at
the Alamo, they turned the tables at the Battle of San Jacinto, near
present-day Houston. This remarkable battle lasted only eighteen
minutes, during which time the outnumbered Texian militiamen
accomplished a complete rout of the Mexican troops. The Mexicans
suffered casualties of 630 killed and 730 taken prisoner; the Texians lost only 9 dead and 30 wounded. Though their independence
from Mexico was not yet recognized by the Mexican government,

the Texians knew they had secured their victory and now controlled the disputed land.

Between the Battle of the Alamo and the Battle of San Jacinto, there took place a violent episode that is mostly overlooked in history books. Three weeks after the downfall of the Alamo, in the small town of Goliad, ninety-three miles southeast of San Antonio, 342 Texian fighters were executed on orders from Gen. Antonio López de Santa Anna, the same man who laid siege to the Alamo. The soldiers did not die as heroes, however, but as victims of their leaders' indecision and incompetence.

Yet out of the Goliad disaster emerged a story of courageous defiance on the part of one young Mexican woman, Francita Alavez, known in the annals of Texas history as the "Angel of Goliad." Her story is the only recorded incident in the Texas Revolution where a Mexican citizen with the Mexican army showed compassion for the avowed enemy.

Little is known about the background of Francita Alavez (both her first and last names are variously spelled). She entered the Texas independence story as an unofficial member of a company led by General José de Urrea, one of Santa Anna's best officers, in February 1836. She traveled as the companion of one of the general's staff, Captain Telesforo Alavez. It remains unclear whether Francita was Alavez's legal wife, his mistress, or a favorite prostitute. While there are no known marriage records, she did carry the captain's name. The survivors of the Goliad tragedy described Francita as perhaps twenty years old, dark-haired, and very beautiful.

Goliad was not Francita's first intercession in the Texian cause. In March 1836 the Mexican army, led by General Urrea, occupied the small settlement of Copano, in today's Refugio County, when an American ship carrying sixty-eight volunteers docked at Copano Bay. Unaware that Copano was in Mexican hands, the men jumped into the water and swam ashore, only to be greeted by armed Mexican soldiers. Taking the new arrivals prisoner, the Mexicans tied them up, more tightly than necessary, and left them in the hot sun without food or water.

This was Francita's first encounter with "gringos." Offended at the harsh treatment they were receiving, she raged at the guards to untie the prisoners and give them food and water. The guards hesitated at first to give comfort to their enemy, but Francita, considered an officer's wife, kept ranting until she wore them down. The gratitude of the American captives impressed her, and from that day forward she would be a thorn in the side of her patriotic and well-respected paramour.

The settlement of Goliad was originally known as La Bahía, Spanish for "the Bay," a name that referred generally to Matagorda Bay. In the 1820s, immediately after Mexico gained its independence from Spain, Anglo-Americans began colonizing the area. At this time, La Bahía was one of three Spanish settlements in Texas, the other two being Bexar (now San Antonio) and Nacogdoches, near the Louisiana border. In 1829 the settlement's name was changed to Goliad, though the presidio (Spanish fort) retained the original name. It was at Presidio La Bahía that the first declaration of Texas independence was read on December 20, 1835, though the declaration wasn't signed until the following March.

One of the main characters in the Goliad story was early Anglo settler James Walker Fannin Jr., who had come to Texas in autumn 1834 and established a plantation near today's Freeport. Fannin, one of the earliest and most dedicated supporters of the fight for Texas independence, was a respected leader in General Sam Houston's militia when he was sent to Goliad in early 1835.

Fannin was sent to Goliad as part of an ambitious but poorly planned Texian campaign to occupy key presidios in Mexico, including the Alamo, La Bahía, and several others. Meanwhile, unknown to the Texians, Santa Anna was already implementing a plan to take over the presidios in Texas. In charge of the campaign was General José de Urrea, one of Santa Anna's most able and trusted officers. While the Texians believed that the Mexican army posed little threat to their own settlements in Mexican Texas, Urrea was already crossing the Rio Grande into the territory. The Texas militiamen would soon find themselves woefully unprepared to fend off the assault.

While Fannin was in Goliad, he sent two of his officers, Francis Johnson and James Grant, to proceed farther with their troops. Within a week, both Johnson and Grant were ambushed by Urrea's army, in both cases losing all but a handful of men.

Meanwhile, when General Houston learned that Santa Anna had entered Texas and was just twenty-five miles south of San Antonio, he instructed the men at the Alamo to vacate the mission. When they refused, he ordered Fannin to reinforce the garrison there. Before he got there, however, Fannin received news of Johnson's defeat and decided to return to Goliad to prepare a defense against the approaching Mexican army.

Back at Goliad, Fannin was ordered to return to San Antonio to assist in the defense of the Alamo, but by the time the troops were ready to march, the mission had already fallen. Houston then directed Fannin to move his army east to Victoria and establish a defensive position there. Fannin, hesitant to abandon his defensive positions at Goliad, delayed his departure and unwittingly sealed his doom.

On March 19, under cover of dense fog, Fannin finally ordered his men out of La Bahía. But the delay was not Fannin's only poor decision. In commencing the march, he ignored Houston's directive to carry only the most vital supplies and artillery, instead overloading the company with cannons and extra wagons. Even worse, he marched without rations for the men.

Later that day near Coleto Creek, less than twenty miles from Goliad, Fannin's company was alerted to the enemy close behind.

Mission chapel, Presidio La Bahía —Author photo

They scurried toward a wooded area but found themselves in a depression in open land, surrounded by Mexican troops. Even though the Texians were without provisions, they held off the better-equipped, better-organized Mexican army until after dark, whereupon General Urrea pulled back to wait for more troops and artillery.

By the next morning, Urrea's reinforcements had arrived at Coleto Creek, and the Mexican forces, on slopes overlooking the Texians' defensive position in the hollow, began to fire. Urrea now had about one thousand men against the defenders' two hundred remaining able-bodied fighters. It didn't take long for Fannin and his men to realize resistance was useless. Still, there was growing disagreement about whether to surrender or fight to the bitter end; many of the officers were concerned about the Mexican military's reputation for barbaric treatment of captured enemies. Finally agreeing to try for an honorable surrender, the Texians sent Fannin out under a white flag with a document of capitulation. The Americans believed that, under the terms of surrender, their wounded would be cared for and that the prisoners would be treated humanely. The Mexican government, however, had a policy of executing nearly all war prisoners as "pirates," though physicians, interpreters, mechanics, or other skilled workers who could serve the Mexican army were sometimes kept alive.

Urrea marched Fannin and the able-bodied soldiers, of which there were about 240, back to Goliad, where some other American prisoners, escapees from the Battle of Refugio, were already being held. Fannin's wounded men, around 80 in number, were transported later. Urrea notified Santa Anna of the Americans' surrender and recommended clemency. Santa Anna angrily refused and ordered that the prisoners be executed immediately. Nevertheless, Urrea asked Colonel José Nicholás de la Portilla, the acting commander at La Bahía, to treat the prisoners with compassion. Portilla, however, knew of Santa Anna's orders and knew he had to follow them.

On the morning of March 27, Palm Sunday, Portilla ordered the prisoners dispersed from the presidio in three different directions. The Americans, led to believe they were going to be set free, were in good spirits. About three-quarters of a mile from La Bahía, in each direction, the guards stopped their prisoners. When their leaders gave commands quickly in Spanish, many of the Texians realized something bad was afoot. The guards encircled the captives, raised their rifles, and fired. The first volley killed all but a few of the Texians. Some ran, but they were pursued and most were shot or stabbed. A few, however, managed to escape into the woods along the San Antonio River; a few others feigned death until the guards left.

Fannin, still inside the fort, was put to death along with about forty other wounded men. Reconciled to his death, he requested that he not be shot in the head and that he be buried. Both requests were ignored. He was shot in the head and thrown on a pile with other slain prisoners. The bodies were burned. The bodies farthest from the presidio were left to the buzzards and wolves. It wasn't until June 3 that a party arrived to secure the remains and bury them. Today a monument stands where Fannin and his men are buried, in one of the largest mass graves on American soil.

Amid the sounds of violent death that fateful Sunday, another voice cried out—that of Francita Alavez.

Upon her arrival at Goliad, just after the battle at Coleto Creek, Francita came face to face with the presidio's "Black Hole," where nearly four hundred prisoners were crammed into a room so small they all had to stand. Seeing these wretched conditions, Francita went immediately to Colonel Portilla and persuaded him to let the captives go out into the courtyard, to give them food, and to permit the doctors among them to treat the wounded. Portilla had been at Copano Bay when Francita helped the captured Americans there, and he had allowed her to talk him out of executing them. He instead had them sent to a prison in Matamoros.

Francita knew that the Goliad prisoners would be killed—in fact, Portilla had shown her the order when it came in. She also knew he had no choice but to follow his instructions. The night before the executions, Francita, under cover of darkness, smuggled about a dozen captives out of the fort and kept them hidden behind the parapet until the coast was clear.

The following morning, Francita, along with several other Mexican women, all dressed in black, stood outside the presidio and watched as the unsuspecting men were marched out. Noticing a fifteen-year-old boy in the line, Francita suddenly ran up and pulled him from the ranks, telling the officer in charge that she needed him in the hospital. For Benjamin Franklin Hughes of Kentucky, the unit's drummer boy, Francita proved to be a guardian angel. Some forty years after the Goliad affair, in an article he wrote about the bloody episode, Hughes attested to Francita's role in saving his life.

Also among the prisoners who were marched out that morning was William Hunter, a volunteer from New Madrid, Missouri. After being shot and stabbed, Hunter was apparently left for dead. He later stated that a beautiful lady named Alavez dragged his body to the riverbank and dressed his wounds.

An estimated 342 men—the majority of the prisoners—were killed at Goliad that day. Twenty-eight managed to escape, and some twenty others—doctors and others with useful skills—were spared. Furthermore, about twenty men and boys—according to historians' best estimates—survived the executions thanks to Francita's intervention.

After the bloodbath, Mexican soldiers came upon seven escapees, killing three and taking the other four alive. The captives were later sent to Victoria, where Captain Alavez had been reassigned. Francita was there when the four prisoners arrived. She watched as they were lined up before a firing squad in the market square. Brazenly, if unwisely, Francita threw herself in front of the Americans. Seeing Francita's bravery, another onlooker, also a Mexican woman, joined Francita and they both refused to move. The execution was canceled.

On April 21, 1836, General Sam Houston led his forces across the San Jacinto plain and routed General Santa Anna and his men. Knowing that the victorious Texan army would soon head south, General Urrea moved his men across the Rio Grande to Matamoros. Among the retreating troops was Telesforo Alavez, with Francita accompanying him.

By some records, shortly after the army's arrival in Matamoros, Telesforo went to Mexico City with Francita and there abandoned her. Sources say that the captain had also abandoned his legal wife, Maria Augustine de Pozo Alavez, along with their two children, in 1834. It is known that Telesforo remained in the Mexican army and retired as a colonel after almost forty years service, but there is nothing more about his private life in any official record.

So what became of the Angel of Goliad? There is evidence that Francita returned to Matamoros homeless and penniless. Some writers claim that the local Mexicans looked upon her sympatheti-cally, but others say that the townspeople spurned her, viewing her compassionate actions as sheer treachery.

A fairly credible account of Francita Alavez's story, including her later years, came to light in the 1930s. Mrs. Elena Zamora

Fannin Monument in Angel of Goliad Plaza, Goliad State Park
—Author photo

O'Shea, a teacher at the Santa Gertrudis Ranch (part of the vast King Ranch empire of south Texas) in 1902 and 1903, wrote in 1936 of meeting an old Mexican man who said he was the grandson of Telesforo Alavez. One day, Mrs. O'Shea was reading aloud about the incident at Goliad when she noticed that one listener, a man called Don Matias Alavez, had become visibly excited. Afterward, he told the teacher about his family.

According to Mrs. O'Shea, Alavez said his grandfather was brought up in the old Mexican tradition in which families arranged marriages. Telesforo had no love for the bride his parents chose for him, and the two separated after a few years. The church granted them an annulment but forbade remarriage. Shortly after his annulment, Telesforo met Francita and fell in love with her. Disregarding the disapproval of both church and family, the couple ran off together.

After the Texian insurrection, Francita and Telesforo settled in Matamoros, where only the captain's prestige kept the locals from ostracizing Francita. When Telesforo died, however, she was immediately shunned.

Two children were born of the couple's union, a boy named Matias and a daughter, Dolores. In 1884 Captain Richard King, who had known Telesforo as well as Francita, offered Matias a job on his Texas ranch, and the family moved to his spread. Some years later Francita died at the ranch, where she was buried in an unmarked grave. Some of her descendants are still associated with the King Ranch.

In 2004 a life-size statue of Francita, along with a marker describing her story, was erected in the Angel of Goliad Plaza in Goliad. At the edge of this plaza, another monument stands over the gravesite of the James W. Fannin and the other men who died at La Bahía. Each year on Palm Sunday, the Angel of Goliad Descendants Historical Preservation organization holds a ceremony here honoring the victims of the massacre.

Another, older monument to Francita Alavez, the only Mexican in the Texas struggle for independence to be honored by the state of Texas, is a bronze bust displayed within the aging, haunted halls of La Bahía. Here at the old mission, where the echoes of long-ago anguish ring against the cold stone walls, one can still feel, rising from the deep shadows, the courageous compassion of a young Mexican woman who thrust herself into the currents of history.

Elisabet Ney, date unknown —Courtesy Texas State
Library and Archives Commission

2

Elisabet Ney

SHE BROUGHT ART TO TEXAS

Although opposed by her parents and the mores of the day, German-born Elisabet Ney was determined to study sculpting. She had to overcome several obstacles in order to enter the Academy of Fine Arts in Munich. First, she conquered her parents' objections by going on a hunger strike until they agreed to let her enroll. Once there, she had to battle the all-male school's reluctance to admit a woman. After allowing her to study there on a trial basis, the academy admitted her in 1852, making Elisabet the first female student in the history of the school. After completing her studies, she opened her own studio in Berlin and soon became a respected artist in Europe.

Always a rebel, Elisabet refused to take her husband's name when she wed, and she usually denied that she was even married. In 1873 she and her husband moved to Texas, where she befriended future governor Oran Roberts. Roberts later encouraged her to resume sculpting, which she did. Her work as well as her support of culture in Austin ushered in a new era of art in Texas.

Elisabet was born Franzisca Bernadina Wilhelmina Elisabeth Ney on January 26, 1833, in Münster, then a city in Prussia but now part of Germany. She had an older brother, Fritz, with whom she

17

often quarreled as a child because he disapproved of her unladylike behavior. Her father, Johann, was an accomplished stonemason, and young Elisabet often worked alongside her father, learning the mechanics of carving stone. Her mother, Anna, was a homemaker, a typical vocation for women of the day. The family was related to one of Napoleon Bonaparte's finest soldiers, French Marshal Michel Ney, who was sometimes referred to as *le brave des braves* ("the bravest of the brave"). Elisabet's independence and steely determination were said to have come from this military side of the family.

In 1853, while she was an art student in Germany, the red-haired, blue-eyed Elisabet met a Scottish medical student named Edmund D. Montgomery. Although they became good friends, Edmund wanted more—namely marriage. Elisabet, however, viewed marriage as enslavement for women, and she refused his proposals for the next ten years. Even so, the two were practically inseparable.

After graduating from the Munich Academy in July 1854, Elisabet moved to Berlin to study under Christian Daniel Rauch, perhaps the best-known sculptor of the mid-nineteenth century. With Rauch she learned to sculpt in the classical German tradition, which favored realism and attention to detail. In 1857 the budding sculptor (she disliked the term sculptress) opened her studio in Berlin.

Soon after entering the male-dominated world of sculpting, Elisabet, with Edmund's help, persuaded an aged Arthur Schopenhauer, the renowned German philosopher, to pose for her. Reluctant at first to sit for a novice sculptor—much less a female one—he was soon won over by Elisabet's charm. The old philosopher began singing her praises to friends and colleagues. As he wrote in one letter, "She is very beautiful and indiscernibly *liebenswürdig* [endearing]." Schopenhauer, through both his friendship and his writings, was a big influence on the young artist.

Elisabet's sculpture of Schopenhauer was received with such acclaim that it quickly led to commissions for other works, including a bust of King George V. She traveled throughout Europe sculpting many prominent people, including Jacob Grimm, of Grimm's Fairy Tales fame; Italian military hero Giuseppe Garibaldi; and Otto von Bismarck, future founder of the German empire.

In 1863 the persistent Edmund finally won his ladylove's hand. On November 7 of that year, he and Elisabet were married on the Portuguese island of Madeira, where Edmund had established a medical practice. Elisabet had relented because Edmund shared her belief in freedom, equality, and the pursuit of self-fulfillment for men and women alike. She made her groom agree to two conditions, however: the marriage would remain a secret, and she would keep her maiden name.

The year the couple married, Edmund was diagnosed with tuberculosis, then known as consumption. He had lived with the condition for some seven years when he received a letter from friends who lived in the state of Georgia. They suggested that the couple immigrate to the American South, where the warm, humid climate was considered therapeutic for consumptives. Later that year, Edmund and Elisabet moved to Thomasville, in southern Georgia, close to the Florida state line. While there, the couple had their first son, Arthur (Artie), in January 1871.

Edmund and Elisabet did not like the conservative atmosphere in Georgia, however, and began to look for a place to settle permanently. Leaving Arthur in the care of a nurse and two servants, they embarked on a trip around the United States to find a new home. In October 1872, Edmund and Elisabet, who was pregnant again, boarded a paddleboat in St. Paul, Minnesota, for a trip down the Mississippi River. While on the boat, Elisabet went into labor. Preferring to have their child on dry land, the couple debarked at Red Wing, a small village in Minnesota, where Elisabet gave birth to the couple's second child, another boy. They named him Lorne, for Edmund's cousin, the Marquis of Lorne, son-in-law of Queen Victoria. Elisabet rested a few days before returning to Georgia.

The hostility of people in Thomasville toward the "unmarried" couple became even worse when the two returned home from their travels with a new baby. According to Ney biographer Marjory Goar, the arrival of "another little bastard" fed fuel to the fire of gossip and disapproval.

Shortly after their return home, Edmund and Elisabet heard about the availability of land in Texas, a state reputed to have fine soil and plenty of water. They were especially interested in the town of Brenham, a German farming community with rail service. The idea of once again being among educated Germans appealed to them. In early 1873, Elisabet went to Texas to scout properties in the Brenham area. Edmund, not feeling well, stayed home with the children.

Upon arriving in Texas, Elisabet visited an 1,100-acre cotton plantation near Hempstead, some twenty miles southeast of Brenham. Instantly enchanted by the place, known as Liendo, she sent word to her husband. The house needed work, but Elisabet relished the thought of fixing it up and restoring it to its former glory. On March 4, 1873, Edmund and Elisabet bought the Liendo Plantation, where they would live for the next twenty years. Elisabet ran the plantation while Edmund resumed his scientific and medical research.

Shortly after the family's move to Liendo, little Arthur died of diphtheria. Elisabet shocked the neighbors when she made a death mask of her dead son and then, to prevent spread of the disease, burned the boy's body instead of giving him a "proper" burial. Elisabet placed Arthur's ashes in a leather pouch, which she hung on a nail by the fireplace. When Edmund died many years later, the pouch was put in his coffin.

Elisabet at Liendo, date unknown —Courtesy
Texas State Library and Archives Commission

Elisabet was not much more popular in Hempstead than she had been in Thomasville. As far as the locals knew, she and Edmund were "living in sin" with illegitimate children. She often wore long, flowing robes, ate no meat, and liked to sleep outdoors in a hammock. In addition to her unorthodox behavior, she had a haughty, unsociable attitude. And she was opinionated. "Women are fools," she is quoted as saying, "to be bothered with housework. Look at me. I sleep in a hammock which requires no making up. I break an egg and sip it raw. I make lemonade in a glass and then rinse it, and my housework is done for the day."

Elisabet did make a few friends, however. In 1878 she and Edmund met Judge Oran Roberts while he was in Hempstead campaigning for governor. Roberts, surprised to discover a renowned

European artist residing in rural Texas, told the couple of his determination to bring art, culture, and higher education to the state. Should he be elected, he told Elisabet, he would like her to help him pursue this goal. She was thrilled at the idea of entering the art world again after so many years. Things at Liendo were not going particularly well at that time. The plantation was not profitable, and debts were beginning to mount. The renovation of the house and grounds was more difficult than she had anticipated, and she had made little progress. Worst of all, her only surviving son, Lorne, was unhappy and beginning to rebel against her. Although Roberts did indeed win the election, it would be several years before Elisabet would get an opportunity to resume her art. In the meantime, she continued to struggle with her troubles at Liendo.

Elisabet's difficulties with Lorne, or Lore as he was called, intensified with each passing year. The boy resented her insistence that he dress in togas and sandals, clothes that were completely out of place in Texas and made him the target of ridicule among his peers. Elisabet eventually gave in and ordered him clothes that were closer to what the other children wore, but Lore had other problems. Because Elisabet did not want her son attending local schools, she hired private tutors, but none of them lasted very long. Lore refused to do his schoolwork and played tricks on the teachers. When he fell in with a bad crowd of bigoted hellions, Elisabet forbade him to associate with them, a move that only drove the two further apart.

In 1883, during Governor Roberts's second term, the Texas capitol was partially destroyed by fire. The legislature approved the governor's plan to build the nation's biggest and most grandiose state capitol. Appointing a committee to study building plans and make recommendations, Roberts invited Elisabet to come to Austin as a design consultant. She quickly accepted. Elisabet appeared at the first committee meeting dressed in a white, Grecian-style toga and white kid gloves. Any eyebrows that may have been raised by the odd outfit were overshadowed by Elisabet's reputation as an artist.

The following year, Edmund decided that the family would spend the rest of their lives in America, and in 1884 he and Elisabet applied for American citizenship. On September 16, 1886, the couple became citizens of the United States.

As Lore entered adolescence, his relationship with his mother continued to deteriorate. When the boy was about fifteen, Edmund finally stepped in and told Elisabet that he wanted to send Lore away to school out of state. Over his wife's strong objections, Edmund decided that Swarthmore, a Quaker school near Philadelphia, was the best place for their son. For his part, Lore jumped at the opportunity to leave Texas.

After a year at Swarthmore, however, Lore had failed to make the grade. His father transferred him to another Quaker-founded school, Chappaqua Mountain Institute in southeastern New York state, but Lore fared no better there. Finally Edmund sent him to an expensive boarding school for boys near Geneva, Switzerland, called Chateau de Laucy. In Europe, Lore became a spendthrift and piled up large debts. When Edmund refused to send him any more money, he ran away from school. A frantic Elisabet contacted a friend from Texas, Mrs. Robert Leisewitz, who was visiting relatives in Germany. Mrs. Leisewitz found Lore in Italy, "broke, lonesome, and glad to see his friends from Texas," and brought him home.

Lore returned to Liendo in January 1892. Oran Roberts arranged for Lore to enroll in the University of Texas School of Law, but it wasn't long before the young man lost interest and dropped out. In July 1893, Elisabet was enraged to learn that Lore had eloped with Daisy Thompkins, the sixteen-year-old daughter of a local judge.

When she later met Daisy face-to-face, Elisabet greeted her new daughter-in-law icily, saying, "So you're the hussy who stole my son." The fierce quarrel that followed ended with Elisabet packing her bags and returning to Austin while Lore and Daisy stayed on at Liendo. The young couple eventually divorced, and Daisy left town with their two children. Lore married two more times, though both wives died. His relationship with his mother never fully healed.

In October 1890, Oran Roberts, who was now a professor of law at the University of Texas, asked Elisabet to come to Austin again, this time to consult with a committee of local women who were planning an exhibit for the 1893 Chicago World's Fair. Edmund chose to stay behind at Liendo. The couple would visit each other often, however, traveling by train between Austin and Hempstead.

Upon her arrival in Austin, Elisabet set up a temporary office in the basement of the capitol. Two years later she built a studio in the Hyde Park neighborhood of central Austin. She named the place Formosa, Portuguese for "beautiful." Later that year, the state legislature allotted $32,000 for Elisabet to sculpt Texas legends Stephen F. Austin and Sam Houston for the Chicago World's Fair. Both statues are now in the state capitol, with copies in the U.S. Capitol in Washington. Also in Washington, the Smithsonian National Museum of American Art houses Elisabet's depiction of Shakespeare's Lady Macbeth, an unusual piece for Ney but one of her favorites.

Elisabet made many friends in Austin, inviting special guests to al fresco dinners on the grounds of Formosa, which was fast becoming the cultural center of the city. Among her famous visitors were tenor Enrico Caruso, pianist Ignacy Paderewski, and ballerina Anna Pavlova. Elisabet would spend the rest of her life thus occupied in the state capital.

Elisabet Ney died of "heart trouble" in Austin on June 29, 1907, at age seventy-four. Edmund had been at her bedside nursing her for a month. Elisabet bequeathed the contents of her studio, Formosa, to the University of Texas at Austin. The studio is now the Elisabet Ney Museum, which houses many of the artist's sculptures. In 1941, the city of Austin assumed ownership of the museum.

Two months after Elisabet's death, Edmund suffered a stroke that left him an invalid until his death on April 11, 1911. His extensive library of scientific and medical works became the property of Southern Methodist University in Dallas. Elisabet and Edmund are buried side by side at Liendo.

As for Lore, he was in an accident in which he suffered a severe and painful spinal injury in early 1913. He died a few months later, leaving five orphaned children. When Lore's youngest child, Elisabet Ney Montgomery Douthit, died in 1964, she was buried beside her namesake grandmother, whom she never knew.

Lizzie Johnson Williams, date unknown —Courtesy
Austin History Center, Austin Public Library

3

Elizabeth Johnson Williams

"CATTLE QUEEN OF TEXAS"

Lizzie Johnson was an independent, educated, self-supporting woman at a time when women were seldom seen in the business world. On her own, she built a cattle empire and amassed a small fortune. She married much later in life than most women of her era, and even then she kept her accounts separate from those of her husband, whose business acumen was dismal compared to hers. She was among a handful of women to travel the grueling Chisholm Trail, and she was the only one known to have driven her own herd under her own brand. Even when adorned in one of her elegant gowns, Lizzie was one tough cookie.

Elizabeth Ellen "Lizzie" Johnson was born in central Missouri on May 9, 1840, the second of seven children born to Thomas and Catherine Johnson. When Lizzie was about four years old, the family moved to Texas. They first settled in Huntsville, then moved to Lockhart, then Webberville, and finally to western Hays County, about twenty miles south of Austin. Thomas Johnson, a devout Presbyterian, chose this relatively remote area to keep his family away from outside wickedness. Here he established a school, the Johnson Institute, in 1852. Thomas taught mathematics, Latin, and general studies, and Catherine served as housemother, cook, and part-time piano teacher. Lizzie and all of her siblings were educated at the institute.

After completing her education at the Johnson Institute, Lizzie attended Chappell Hill Female College, in western Washington County. Receiving her degree in 1859, Lizzie returned home and taught at the institute. Four years later, Lizzie left her parents' school to teach elsewhere. After Lizzie's father died in 1868, her brother Ben took over operation of the school for a few years, but he closed it in 1873.

After leaving the Johnson Institute, Lizzie taught in various schools in the Austin area. Some records indicate that she was a tough disciplinarian, and in at least one instance at the Johnson Institute, she had the community up in arms over her severe treatment of one of her students. Yet she was still teaching in Austin as late as 1880.

In addition to teaching, Lizzie earned extra money bookkeeping for local ranchers and writing articles, under an unknown pen name, for such publications as *Leslie's Illustrated Weekly*. Shrewd, intuitive, and gifted in financial matters, she saved her earnings to invest in cattle. She had learned much about the cattle business through her bookkeeping jobs, paying close attention to the ranchers' day-to-day operations and talking with successful cattlemen in the area. Around 1868 she bought $2,500 worth of stock in the Evans, Snider, Bewell Cattle Company of Chicago. Three years later, she sold the stock for $20,000.

Using some of this money, Lizzie entered the cattle business in earnest. On June 1, 1871, she registered a cattle brand in her own name. Two days later, she paid rancher Charles W. Whitis $3,000 in gold for ten acres of land near Austin, where she began to raise her own herds. Even though she was a successful rancher, she also continued teaching for a while. In 1873 Lizzie bought a two-story house in Austin, converting the first floor into a school and maintaining her living quarters upstairs. In the meantime, her cattle business continued to grow.

By the late 1870s, Lizzie Johnson had become known as the "Cattle Queen of Texas." On June 8, 1879, at age thirty-nine, the wealthy Lizzie married widower Hezekiah G. "Hez" Williams, a former Baptist minister turned rancher with seven children. In a highly unusual move for the time, Lizzie had Hez sign a premarital contract, in which he agreed that all of her assets would remain in her name. It is unclear whether Lizzie knew that her groom had problems with drinking, gambling, and general dishonesty. One of Lizzie's brothers once quipped that "while the Reverend Williams

Wedding photo of Hezekiah and Lizzie Williams, June 8, 1879
—Courtesy Austin History Center, Austin Public Library

was preaching his Sunday sermons, his sons were out stealing the congregation's cattle." According to some sources, Lizzie herself appropriated unbranded cattle during the Civil War. In any case, the marriage lasted—and reportedly thrived—until Hezekiah's death in 1914.

Shortly after her marriage, Lizzie finally gave up teaching to concentrate on her cattle operations. She spent little time at the ranch, however, instead working out of the couple's home in Austin. There is little doubt that Lizzie was the brains behind the couple's cattle business. Hez was not the world's smartest businessman—he gambled a lot and usually lost money on his cattle deals. In comparison, Lizzie, who made a point of keeping her cattle separate from her husband's, always made a profit. Whenever she lent Hez money, she made him sign a note to repay the loan.

Sometime between 1879 and 1885, Lizzie rode with her herd on at least one cattle drive along the Chisholm Trail. Many sources say she made the arduous trip several times. Other women are known to have ridden the trail, and some, such as Amanda Burks and Margaret Borland, did so before Lizzie, but Lizzie was the only one to run her own cattle under her own brand, as opposed to her husband's. Hez rode with her, driving his own stock.

Cattle drives on the Chisholm Trail were a short-lived phenomenon, lasting only from about 1867 to 1885. Yet the Chisholm Trail drives have been called the greatest migration of livestock in world history. During this short period, the trail felt the hoof beats of more than five million cattle and a million mustangs. The trail and its denizens created an iconic image that exists to this day: the cowboy, tall in the saddle and larger than life, riding hard all day on the lonely prairie and camping under the stars, always on the lookout for dangerous outlaws, Indians, and wild animals.

The unusual presence of a woman on the trail fascinated the cowboys who rode with Lizzie. They doted on her, bringing her treats such as wild fruit, prairie chicken, and antelope tongue. But Lizzie was not along just for the ride, nor was she pampered. She was usually up working before the cattle began to stir in the morning. She maintained a daily log of the stock, the trail hands' work, expenditures, and other details. When the herd reached the end of the trail, she kept careful records of each animal sold. Some historians maintain that Lizzie and Hez had a friendly rivalry regarding their separate herds. It was said that they would steal each other's unbranded cattle and mark them with their own brand—and Lizzie usually ended up with the best ones.

As their cattle business continued to grow, Lizzie and Hezekiah began to enjoy the fruit of their labors, often traveling to St. Louis, Kansas City, and New York and staying at the best hotels. In Texas, Lizzie was sensible in her dress and stern in her behavior, but in the big city she lived the high life, socializing with wealthy cattlemen and their wives and wearing the latest fashions. Her city outfits were often opulent, made of velvet, silk, and brocade, trimmed with lace and braiding, and accessorized with expensive jewelry. Once, while in New York, Lizzie spent $10,000 on jewelry alone.

Sometime around the dawn of the twentieth century, Lizzie and Hezekiah spent a few years conducting business in Cuba, which was at the time a newly emerging market for beef. While there, Hezekiah was kidnapped and a ransom of $50,000 was demanded for his release. Lizzie paid it without blinking an eye. Some have speculated that Hezekiah arranged the kidnapping himself to put some money in his pocket. Others claim that Lizzie made him sign all his property over to her in exchange for the ransom payment. While documents verify that Hez's assets were to be transferred to Lizzie on July 30, 1896, the reason for this exchange is unknown, and the papers were not recorded, for whatever reason, until about 1913, after Hez had become very ill.

In 1908 the courthouse in San Marcos, the Hays County seat, burned down. Hezekiah saw this as an excellent opportunity to found his own city and create a new county seat. With Lizzie's support, Hez built a town on their ranch, some twelve miles north of San Marcos. He laid out lots for the town, which he christened Hays City, and built a hotel, a church, and a livery stable. The effort proved to be an exercise in futility. San Marcos was an established city with a secure power base, and the couple found no support for their scheme. There is very little left of Hays City today.

When Hezekiah's health began to fail a few years later, Lizzie took him to a spa resort in Hot Springs, Arkansas, where the natural mineral waters were believed to have healing powers. The trip did no good. They next went to the warm sunshine of El Paso, but that did not help either. It appeared that Hez's lifelong drinking problem was finally taking its toll.

Hez died in El Paso in 1914, and Lizzie had his body brought back to Austin. She paid $600 for a coffin (about $13,000 in today's money). When she paid the mortician's bill, she scrawled across the bottom, "I loved this old buzzard this much." The couple had no children of their own, and though Hezekiah had children with his first wife, Lizzie was the sole heir to his estate.

Following Hezekiah's death, Lizzie—never a social butterfly in Austin—became a virtual recluse and often dressed in shabby clothes. People began to call her eccentric, and she earned a reputation as a miser. She lived in a small apartment in a building she owned, the Brueggerhof, and rented out the other units. If her tenants asked for firewood, she doled it out one stick at a time. When the cafe across the street raised the price of soup a few pennies, Lizzie, in her own crafty way, made a deal with the owner to keep paying the original ten cents for her soup.

Despite her advancing age, Lizzie continued to conduct her own business affairs. She always paid her bills right away. Once, when a bank note for several thousand dollars came due, she walked into the bank, sat down at the bank officer's desk, and pulled out a red bandana full of cash, from which she counted out the amount to the penny.

Lizzie could still be her old flamboyant self when she wanted to. In 1916, at age seventy-six, she showed up at her nephew's wedding in a carriage drawn by two white horses, emerging in full regalia, including a diamond tiara.

When her health began to deteriorate and she could no longer look after herself, Lizzie reluctantly agreed to move in with her sister's daughter, Willie Greer Shelton, and her husband, John, in Austin. Her niece took good care of her, and she lived to be eighty-four.

Lizzie Johnson Williams died on October 9, 1924. She was interred in Austin's Oakwood Cemetery. Curiously, she left no will. Because of her unkempt appearance and penny-pinching ways in her later years, many people were surprised to learn that her estate was valued at about $250,000 (over $3 million in today's currency). Much of Lizzie's wealth was not discovered until almost two years after her death, when relatives found in her apartment thousands of dollars in cash, checks, and gold scattered carelessly among her papers, as well as diamond jewelry wrapped in an old piece of cloth. She also had bank accounts with significant sums and land holdings throughout Texas.

Her greatest legacy, however, was not the money she left behind, but her mark on Texas history. More than just a "Cattle Queen," Lizzie Johnson Williams was a true pioneer for women.

"Aunt Mollie" Bailey in her later years, date unknown —Courtesy
Western History Collections, University of Oklahoma Libraries

4
Mollie Kirkland Bailey

CIRCUS OWNER, NURSE, MOTHER, AND SPY

In the late nineteenth century, about the time Barnum & Bailey's "Greatest Show on Earth" was making a name for itself, a smaller circus was playing venues around Texas. Bailey's Circus (no relation to Barnum & Bailey) was in its own way just as successful as its famous competitor. It had started as a husband-and-wife effort, but the wife—"Aunt Mollie" Bailey—eventually took over full operation of the circus. Strong and independent, Mollie was a respected businesswoman. But over her lifetime, she had also been much more: wife, mother, performer, nurse, and Confederate spy.

As far as historians can tell, Mollie Arline Kirkland was born on November 2, 1844, on a plantation in Sumter County, Alabama. By age twelve, she was, according to a biography by her daughter-in-law Olga, a beautiful young girl with a "gypsy-like appearance, dark hair, flashing black eyes, and a vivacious manner . . . a graceful, charming young lady, a belle of the day." Had she followed the wishes of her parents, William and Mary, Mollie would have married a wealthy, aristocratic man and become a Southern woman of stature. Mollie, however, had different plans.

At age fourteen, while home from her private boarding school, Mollie met the person who would change the course of her life forever. That person was Gus Bailey, the musician son of a circus owner. After seeing him in the circus, Mollie fell head over heels for the redheaded traveling troubadour. The pair wanted to marry (fourteen was a marriageable age in the South at that time), but Mollie's father refused to allow it, believing Gus to be a highly unsuitable match for his well-bred daughter. The strong-willed Mollie, however, disregarded her father's wishes, and on March 21, 1858, she became Mrs. Gus Bailey, joining her husband on the circuit. Upon learning of the wedding, Mollie's father disowned her, and the two never reconciled.

Intelligent, ambitious, and tenacious, Mollie soon convinced her husband that they should form their own show. Gus agreed, but the pair had limited financial resources. Though seldom dishonest, Mollie sneaked back to her family's plantation one night and purloined some of her father's horses and wagons. The couple then took to the road.

Along with Gus's brother and Mollie's half-sister, the Baileys started a traveling vaudeville act they called the Bailey Family Troupe. Traveling through Alabama, Arkansas, and Mississippi, they performed wherever they could find an audience. Gus was an all-around performer—comedian, actor, fiddler, and bandleader. Mollie performed as an actress, singer, and organist. Gus's brother, Alfred, was a musician and a contortionist, the latter always a big draw in small rural communities. Fannie Kirkland, Mollie's half-sister, was an actress and dancer.

On May 21, 1861, just weeks after the outbreak of the Civil War, Gus enlisted in the Confederate Army in Selma, Alabama. He ended up in Company Thirteen of the Arkansas Infantry, part of John Bell Hood's Texas Brigade. Gus was made leader of the Third Arkansas Band and played with a group of musicians and actors known as Hood's Minstrels. It was during the Civil War that he penned "The Old Gray Mare," a ditty still familiar to older generations. The song became a military march and, much later, it was chosen as the official song of the 1928 Democratic National Convention in Houston.

Mollie, too, did her part for the war effort. She had recently given birth to a daughter, Dixie, the first of nine children. Leaving the baby with friends in Richmond, Virginia, Mollie served as a nurse wherever she was needed. When the troops went into winter quarters, she and Fannie joined Gus at his fort and performed with Hood's Minstrels, singing and dancing to entertain the soldiers. Her expertise as a thespian, coupled with nerves of steel, served her well in another role—that of Confederate spy.

A good number of women on both sides acted as spies during the Civil War. Female spies had several advantages over their male counterparts. Just being a woman deflected suspicion, since women were seldom seen as security threats. They often posed as disinterested servants or nurses, crossing enemy lines undisturbed and going other places a combatant would not be able to go. They could infiltrate social situations and pick up information from unguarded conversation. Furthermore, due to standards of propriety, they could easily hide messages or supplies in their skirts, hair, or bonnets with little chance of being searched. If captured, females were rarely executed but only sent to prison.

On one of her spy forays, Mollie dressed as an old woman doling out cookies to Yankee soldiers. Thus disguised, Mollie not only penetrated the Union pickets, but remained among the enemy troops for a time. Virtually invisible to the soldiers, she was able to gather a wealth of helpful information before returning to the Confederate camp.

Also during the war, Mollie once undertook a perilous trip through enemy lines for humanitarian rather than espionage purposes. Medicine, especially quinine, was in short supply, but in order to deliver some to the soldiers of the Third Arkansas Infantry, she would have to travel to and from the nearest Confederate hospital through risky territory. By hiding packets of quinine powder in her pompadour hairdo, she made the trip safely, helping many sick soldiers. The plan worked so brilliantly that one officer quipped, "Depend on a woman to think up a good scheme."

After the war, much of the country, especially the South, was destitute. The Baileys were no different. Also, like many other war veterans, Gus had contracted a respiratory illness, probably consumption (tuberculosis), from spending cold, damp nights on the ground. On top of this, he and Mollie now had three young daughters to care for. In desperation the Baileys took low-paying and creatively limited jobs as performers on a showboat. During this time, Mollie had four more children, all sons. Two more girls were born later. Of the nine kids, three daughters died as young children. The surviving children—Birda (or Birdie), Eugene (James Eugene), Allie (George Albertine), Willie (William Kirkland), Brad (Brad Scott), and Minnie—all eventually joined the show.

As soon as they were able, around 1876, the Baileys quit the showboat tour to form the Bailey Concert Company, touring their preferred territory of small towns and rural areas of the South. By then, the older children had joined the act. Over time, the concert company slowly evolved into a circus, a type of show that was just beginning to develop into its modern form. The Baileys moved by wagon from site to site and pitched tents for the show, which included trapeze flyers, acrobats, song-and-dance acts, comedians, sideshow amusements, and a band. Unlike some of the traveling medicine shows and sideshows of the era, the Bailey Company offered wholesome entertainment for a fair price. Gus's brother Alfred was responsible for keeping the circus family-friendly. No drinking was allowed on the premises, and employees were forbidden to curse.

In 1876, after forming the Bailey Concert Company, the Baileys bought a home in Prescott, Arkansas, as a place to stay during

Mollie Kirkland Bailey, circa 1870s[?] —Courtesy Austin History Center, Austin Public Library

the off-season. By this time, Gus's debilitating illness had begun to take its toll, so the operation of the family business fell squarely on Mollie's capable shoulders. Now in her early thirties, Mollie was, according to biographer Martha Hertzog, a "short, rounded figure of a woman, with a small waist and a positive walk." Serving on the front line during the Civil War, giving birth to nine children, and traveling almost constantly with her family business would have taken much out of Mollie, mentally and physically. It is a tribute to her vitality and fortitude that her personality changed very little over the years.

Though they were comfortable in Arkansas, Mollie and Gus had for some time wanted to move to Texas, where numerous settlers were finding homes amid the wide-open spaces. The Baileys had fallen in love with Texas—and Texans—during their wartime stint with Hood's Texas Brigade. Finally, in 1885, the Baileys bought a home in Dallas. Two years after moving to the Lone Star State, the Bailey production became a full-fledged circus in the modern sense of the word, with exotic animals, clowns, and acts performed in a ring. Proud of its new home, the Bailey Circus adopted the slogan "A Texas Show for Texas People." In a reflection of the times, three flags flew from the tent poles: the U.S. Stars and Stripes, the Lone Star of Texas, and the Confederate Stars and Bars.

Though their show had grown bigger, Mollie and Gus continued to play only small, rural towns. What they may have missed in profits, they made up for in audience loyalty. Farmers, small-time merchants, school kids, and other rural denizens flocked to see the Bailey Circus when it came to their area each year. The tour usually left Dallas in the spring, traveling through eastern Texas, then on to southern Texas. After that the troupe turned north, stopping at various sites in the Dallas area. From there, the circus wended its way through West Texas, then turned north to the Panhandle, finally returning to Dallas in December for its winter hiatus.

Gus's bad health finally caught up with him in 1890, forcing him to retire to Blum, a small community southwest of Dallas. He died six years later. For years people had been referring to the circus as the Mollie Bailey Show; when Gus retired, the name became official.

From the time Gus became sick, Mollie had increasingly been handling the management of the business. She had to map out routes, organize the acts, pay expenses, and handle the myriad other details that go into running a major enterprise. One of the operation's biggest expenses was the cost of leasing space for the shows. Realizing that in many cases it was cheaper to buy a piece of land than to pay the high taxes associated with renting entertainment space, Mollie, ever the shrewd entrepreneur, simply purchased land in many of the towns on the circus's regular schedule. When the circus was away, Mollie let the townspeople use the lots as playing fields or picnic grounds, or for other community activities. Thus Mollie Bailey actively contributed to the communities in which her circus appeared. Appreciative Texans affectionately began calling her "Aunt Mollie."

Mollie put much of the show's profits into charitable endeavors, including Confederate memorials and numerous church buildings. She always granted free entry to the circus for war veterans, regardless of which color uniform they had worn. She also gave free passes to each community's poorer children.

When each show opened, Mollie would stand at the tent entrance and personally greet the audience members. The show began with the blast of a trumpet, followed by the clowns. One of them was always dressed as a woman and "flirted" with some of the men in the crowd. After the clowns warmed up the audience, the performers entered in an opening parade. Birda, the Baileys' youngest daughter, rode in on a black horse, and behind her a string of Shetland ponies pulled a carriage full of trained birds. Next came more animals, including, after 1902, a camel and an elephant. Allie and Brad, two of the Bailey boys, began the show, performing high-wire acts. Despite the risk of falling to their death, the Baileys never faltered. Next were the trained animal acts—Birda's birds, Allie's dogs, and Brad's ponies. Singing, dancing, and skits rounded out the evening.

When Mollie Bailey's colorful wagons and motley menagerie rode into town, schools dismissed students for half a day to enjoy the show, and Civil War veterans made a point of lining up to shake hands with Aunt Mollie. Townspeople and statesmen alike

Mollie Bailey with circus wagons, date unknown —Courtesy
Western History Collections, University of Oklahoma Libraries

attended the performances. Governor James Stephen Hogg once presented Mollie with a gold-mounted wild boar's tooth (from a boar he had shot) with her name inscribed on it; she wore it as a brooch.

Among her other accomplishments, Mollie is often credited with bringing Texas its first motion picture, which was shown in a smaller tent adjacent to the big top. The film's subject was the 1898 sinking of the battleship *Maine* in Havana, Cuba, a precipitating event of the Spanish-American War.

In 1906 the Baileys' circus changed its mode of transportation from wagons to trains, skipping over many of its smaller venues and losing much of its original character. To ensure the company rode in style, Mollie bought two Pullman cars for the troupe and a plush parlor car for herself, in which she entertained many well-known Texas figures of the day, including governors Branch

Colquitt and James Hogg, as well as various legislators. Former members of Hood's Texas Brigade were always welcome in the parlor car, where conversation flowed and old war stories were recalled at length.

It was also in 1906 that Mollie married A. H. "Blackie" Hardesty. Although Blackie's age at the time was not recorded, it is known that he was much younger than sixty-two-year-old Mollie. Due to Mollie's fame, it wasn't long before people began referring to him as Blackie Bailey. Blackie gradually took over management of the circus, though Mollie still pulled the strings.

In 1917 Birda became ill and Mollie moved to Houston to take care of her. She still controlled the circus, however, keeping in daily contact through telephone calls, telegrams, and letters. But even after Birda died in September 1917, Mollie did not return to the circus. The following year she fell and broke her hip, a serious injury from which she was unable to recover. She died from complications on October 2, 1918, and was buried in Hollywood Cemetery in Houston. Aunt Mollie's energy was so legendary that some people said her heart kept beating for two hours after her death.

After their mother's death, the four Bailey sons—Allie, Brad, Eugene, and Willie—along with Blackie, continued with the circus for a while, but they lacked Mollie's passion and business acumen. It was one of Mollie's few failings that she had trained no one to really manage the business, and the circus soon folded. The boys wandered off in different directions, and Blackie became a bus driver near Houston.

About thirty years after the Mollie Bailey Show closed down, the better-known and much larger Ringling Brothers and Barnum & Bailey Circus lowered its tent for the last time, on July 16, 1956. Later, under new management, the circus reopened without the big top; the shows were instead performed in indoor arenas, civic centers, and the like. Another classic of American culture had faded away.

Mollie Bailey and her thrilling shows were not forgotten in rural Texas. Biographer Herzog relates the story of a woman in Coolidge, Texas, who in 1952 recalled the devotion her husband and son had shown for Mollie Bailey over the years. "When she asked her husband why he persisted in seeing the same old show over and over, he replied, 'She is everything a show should be—clean, wholesome, no shin games. She's . . . well, she's Mollie Bailey, and I'm going to her show as long as it comes over the road.'"

That is a great memorial for anyone.

Clara Driscoll, date unknown —Courtesy
Daughters of the Republic of Texas Library

5

Clara Driscoll

"SAVIOR OF THE ALAMO"

Clara Driscoll, born into wealth and
privilege, put her affluence to great service.
In Texas, she supported the arts, hospitals, and
especially historic preservation. She was also very active in state
and national politics, working for Democratic candidates and progressive causes. But of all her contributions, she is best known for
her work to preserve and restore the San Antonio de Valero Mission, commonly known as the Alamo.

Clara was born April 2, 1881, to Robert and Julia Driscoll in St.
Mary's, Texas, near Bayside, some twenty-five miles north of Corpus Christi. She had one brother, Robert Jr., who was ten years older.
Clara's hometown is now a ghost town, no longer shown on most
state maps. Her ancestors were Irish pioneers who settled the area,
and both of her grandfathers fought in the Texas Revolution.

By 1890 Clara's father had accumulated a fortune in banking,
commercial development, and ranching, mostly in the Corpus
Christi area. He wanted his only daughter to be well educated and
cultured, so he sent Clara to private boarding schools in Texas,
New York City, and France. She was away from home for about
ten years of her youth, growing into a fiery, auburn-haired beauty.
After completing her studies in 1899, Clara was touring Europe
with her mother, Julia, when Julia suddenly became ill and died in

London. Clara returned to Texas grief-stricken but determined to make a life for herself in her home state.

Clara's foreign travels had imbued in her a deep sense of history. She felt that historic sites in Texas should be preserved for future generations to enjoy. One of these was the Alamo. On a visit to San Antonio shortly after she came home, Clara was appalled at the appearance of the former mission's buildings and grounds. The chapel, maintained by the city of San Antonio, was deteriorating, and the monastery/barracks and courtyard, privately owned, were in even worse condition.

In Clara's eyes, the Battle of the Alamo represented the epitome of people's fight for freedom. The battle had been fought only sixty-three years earlier, yet it already seemed that people had forgotten the sacrifices that took place there. She noted that the mission "was in such a state that strangers seeing it for the first time asked, with obvious disappointment in their voices, 'Is *that* the Alamo?'"

Following the famous 1836 battle, the Alamo stood empty until the end of the Mexican-American War in 1848, when federal troops occupied the fortified mission. Then, with the start of the Civil War, the troops left for other garrisons. When that conflict ended in 1865, federal troops returned to the Alamo, where they stayed until they moved to the newly built Fort Sam Houston in 1875. Although the state of Texas had purchased the mission's chapel in 1883, the barracks and the grounds were used by commercial concerns for the next two decades.

When Clara arrived on the scene, the owner of the barracks and grounds was a wholesale-merchandise firm called Hugo & Schmalzer Company. Already distressed by the site's condition, Clara learned in early 1903 that the owners were planning to sell the Alamo property to some St. Louis investors who wanted to convert it into a hotel. Horrified at the thought of losing this historic treasure, she leapt into action. She joined the Daughters of the

Republic of Texas (DRT), which was trying to acquire the Alamo for the state of Texas and preserve it as a historic site. The process would prove to be a two-year struggle for Clara and the DRT.

The DRT, still in existence, is a historic-preservation group composed of female direct descendants of the pioneers who established the Republic of Texas. It was formed in 1891 through the leadership of Betty Ballinger and Hally Bryan. By the time Clara joined the organization, the DRT had already succeeded in spearheading several projects that honored Texas history, including lobbying the state legislature to buy and preserve the site of the Battle of San Jacinto.

Clara and Adina de Zavala, president of the DRT's San Antonio chapter and granddaughter of the republic's first vice president, Lorenzo de Zavala, found out that Hugo & Schmalzer was asking $75,000 for the barracks and yard. The first $5,000 would secure the buyers a one-year option, after which time they would have to pay off the balance in yearly installments. The property would also require additional funds for restoration and maintenance. But the DRT had very little money. Just getting the first $5,000, which was needed right away if the women were to beat out the St. Louis developers, was a tall order.

To try to buy some time, Clara approached Hugo & Schmalzer about alternatives. The partners bent only a little, offering a thirty-day option for $500, with the rest, a payment of $4,500, due at the end of the thirty days. They insisted that if the DRT wanted to secure the deal, the $500 had to be paid immediately. The following day, March 18, 1903, Clara handed the two men her personal check for $500. This meant that the DRT had only thirty days to raise the rest of the money or forfeit the property as well as Clara's $500 deposit.

The very next day, the DRT called a membership meeting at the Menger Hotel, adjacent to the Alamo. Clara was appointed chairperson of the fundraising committee, which quickly issued a "Plea for the Alamo" to be mailed to Texans throughout the state, requesting donations of fifty cents and the names and addresses of three friends who might also donate. In addition, Clara appeared in person before the Texas legislature asking for $5,000 in state funding.

The legislature agreed to add the money to its appropriation bill, but the funds would not be available before the April 17 deadline. In the meantime, the DRT's solicitation effort had yielded only $1,021.75, less than one-fourth of the amount needed. Possibly hampering contributions was the fact that most people mistakenly believed that the Alamo already belonged to the state of Texas. It was hard to explain that while the state owned the church building, the barracks and the grounds where Jim Bowie, Davy Crockett, and William B. Travis died were in private hands.

With the deadline approaching, it was clear that the DRT would not have enough for the option payment, leaving the organization in a quandary. Clara once again stepped in to save the day, writing another personal check for the balance. But the women were not out of the woods yet. The option would run until February 10, 1904, at which point they would need to pay the next installment, a daunting sum of $20,000. The DRT would have to raise an average of $2,000 a month for the next ten months. The ladies had their work cut out for them.

In May 1903 the Texas legislature passed the $5,000 appropriation addendum, but less than two weeks later, Governor S. W. T. Lanham vetoed it, worried that the money would be wasted if the deal fell through later. Clara and the other members of the DRT were, understandably, extremely discouraged at this turn of events. Now it was up to them to raise the entire amount.

The women organized potluck dinners, rummage sales, and other events to raise funds. During the annual "Battle of Flowers" festival celebrating the anniversary of the Battle of San Jacinto, the DRT set up a booth in front of the Alamo to solicit donations. Members also organized a competition among their local chapters to see who could raise the most money. In addition, Adina de Zavala and others started a publicity campaign in Texas newspapers. Despite all these efforts, however, the campaign raised less than $6,000. The February 1904 deadline was looming, and the DRT was still far short of its goal. Most DRT members were ready to throw in the towel. All except one, that is: Clara Driscoll.

Clara decided that she would purchase the property herself. She wrote another personal check to cover the more than $14,000 the DRT still needed to make the payment. Furthermore, Clara agreed to pay the rest of the purchase price over five years, signing five notes for $10,000 each. She even agreed to pay for the taxes and insurance. Clara also added a stipulation to the contract: "It is distinctly understood that this property is purchased by Clara Driscoll for the use and benefit of the Daughters of the Republic of Texas, and is to be used by them for the purpose of making a park about the Alamo, and for no other purpose whatsoever."

When Clara's benevolent action was made public, a sudden outpouring of support for the Alamo arose. Newspapers dubbed her the "Savior of the Alamo." One prominent judge led a charge to have the state purchase the property and reimburse Clara. The public clamored to see it done.

As a result, a group of legislators introduced a bill to purchase the Alamo property. It passed and was signed by Governor Lanham on January 26, 1905. The act appropriated $65,000 to reimburse Clara and purchase the property for the state. It also decreed that the DRT should serve as the custodian of all the Alamo buildings and grounds.

The formal transfer of the property title to the state took place on September 5, 1905. A month later, Governor Lanham officially

The Alamo, after restoration —Courtesy Daughters of the Republic of Texas Library

turned custody of the Alamo property over to the Daughters of the Republic of Texas, who promised to maintain it "in good order and repair, without charge to the State."

In 1927, the DRT placed a bronze plaque at the Alamo commemorating Clara Driscoll's generous act. It reads:

LEST WE FORGET

Title to the Alamo Mission property, acquired through her efforts and her personal fortune, was conveyed by CLARA DRISCOLL to the State of Texas, Sept. 5, 1905: "That the sacred shrine be saved from the encroachments of commercialism and stand through eternity a monument incomparable to the immortal heroes who died that Texas might not perish."

Philanthropy and historic preservation were not Clara's only interests. She was also a writer. In 1905 she published a novel, *The Girl of La Gloria*, and the following year a collection of short stories entitled *In the Shadow of the Alamo* was released. She also wrote a comic opera called *Mexicana*, which she produced on Broadway.

During this busy period, in 1906, Clara married Texas legislator and journalist Henry "Hal" Sevier at St. Patrick's Cathedral in New York City. The two had met in Austin while he was a representative. With Hal's term almost up, the couple moved to New York, where Hal became the financial editor of the *New York Sun*, and Clara served as president of the Texas Club. As to be expected of people of their station, the Seviers enjoyed an active life, frequently entertaining guests at their luxurious home on Long Island.

After Clara's father died in 1914, the Seviers returned to Texas to help Clara's brother, Robert, oversee the Driscoll family's vast enterprises. The couple settled in Austin and got back to work. With his experience at the *New York Sun*, Hal established a local newspaper, the *Austin American* (today's *Austin American-Statesman*). Clara continued her good works with various organizations, including the Pan American Round Table (PART), a woman's group that encourages "mutual understanding, knowledge, and friendship among the peoples of the Western Hemisphere." Clara also served as president of the DRT.

In 1916 Clara supervised construction of the couple's new home, Laguna Gloria (Heavenly Lagoon), on the shore of Lake Austin. The design was based on a villa Clara and Hal saw on Lake Como, Italy, during their honeymoon. Stephen F. Austin, the "Father of Texas," once owned the land on which the villa sits. An excellent gardener, Clara oversaw the landscaping of the neglected grounds, which were transformed into a pleasing mixture of natural topography and formal gardens.

When Clara's brother, Robert Driscoll Jr., died in 1929, it fell to Clara to tend the family's vast land and petroleum investments, so she and Hal closed Laguna Gloria and moved to the Driscoll family's ranch west of Corpus Christi. The properties Clara supervised soon doubled in value despite the Great Depression. While managing the estate, she also held the position of president of the Corpus Christi Bank & Trust Company.

In addition to her business and philanthropic work, Clara devoted some of her energies to politics. Throughout her life, she was an avid and active Democrat. She was elected as the party's national committeewoman from Texas in 1922, a position she held for a remarkable sixteen years. In 1940 she helped campaign for Texas native John Nance Garner in his bid for the Democratic nomination against Franklin Roosevelt, though she supported Roosevelt in his run for a fourth term four years later.

Hal, too, was involved in politics. Although he did not run again for public office after serving his two terms in the Texas legislature in the early 1900s, he did work for the government in several capacities. During World War I, he was sent to South America as a member of the Committee on Public Information. In 1933 President Roosevelt appointed Hal ambassador to Chile, and the Seviers moved to Santiago. Although his term at the embassy was not supposed to end until 1937, Hal resigned in 1935 amid rumors of poor health, and the Seviers went back to Texas. Shortly after their return, for unknown reasons, Hal and Clara separated, ending their thirty-one-year marriage in 1937. Hal died three years later. The couple had no children.

Following her divorce, Clara reverted to her maiden name and continued her business and charitable endeavors in Texas. In 1942, as a memorial to her brother, Clara constructed the twenty-story

Robert Driscoll Hotel in Corpus Christi, where she occupied the large penthouse. In 1943 she donated her former home, Laguna Gloria, to the Texas Fine Arts Association to be used as a museum.

Clara Driscoll died of a cerebral hemorrhage on July 17, 1945, at age sixty-four. Her body lay in state at the Alamo chapel, where

This undated portrait of Clara Driscoll by Marjorie Caldwell hangs in the Alamo museum. —Courtesy Daughters of the Republic of Texas Library

the flag was flown at half-mast while thousands came to pay their respects. She was then interred beside her father and brother in the family mausoleum at the Masonic Cemetery in San Antonio. Even after her death, Clara continued her philanthropy, leaving the majority of her estate for the establishment and maintenance of the Driscoll Foundation Children's Hospital in Corpus Christi.

Two weeks after Clara's passing, *Time* magazine published a tribute to her entitled "Empress Clara." "Even for Texas," the article opened, "a woman like Clara Driscoll was something." Her friend Mary Lasswell remembered her as "a great lady in the grand Texas tradition."

Clara Driscoll remains a beloved figure in Texas. The museum at the Alamo exhibits photographs of her along with some of her personal items, and the building's Clara Driscoll Theater was named in her honor. In 1978 the Texas Historical Commission erected a marker at the Masonic Cemetery describing Clara's many accomplishments. And in Austin, among the portraits of famous Texans hanging in the Senate chamber of the Texas Capitol is that of Clara Driscoll, "Savior of the Alamo."

Minnie Fisher Cunningham, circa 1915 —Courtesy
Texas State Library and Archives Commission

6

Minnie Fisher Cunningham

"MINNIE FISH"

Minnie Fisher Cunningham worked hard and overcame a number of obstacles to become one of the first women in Texas to receive an advanced degree in pharmacy. Of the fourteen graduates in her 1901 class, she was the only woman, and only the sixth woman in history to earn a graduate degree in pharmacy. But after only one year as a prescription clerk in a Huntsville, Texas, drugstore, Minnie walked out. She was paid $75 a month, while the male clerks were paid $150, even though she had a degree. That pay inequity "made a suffragette out of me," Minnie said.

A suffragette, or suffragist, was a supporter of women's right to vote, but in those days the term also had a broader meaning—most suffragettes supported women's rights in general; today we would call Minnie a feminist. Although she was never elected to a political office, Minnie Fisher Cunningham did make a name for herself as an outspoken champion for civil rights.

Minnie Sue Fisher was born on March 19, 1882, on her family's farm outside New Waverly, Texas, about fifty miles north of Houston. Her parents, Horatio and Sallie Fisher, were struggling farmers. Horatio was also a politician, serving in the Texas House of Representatives in 1857–58. He introduced Minnie to politics by taking her to populist rallies in Huntsville, a few miles up the road from New Waverly.

Sallie Fisher, devoted to education, homeschooled her eight children until they were teenagers. To further their education, she sold dairy products and produce to raise money for private-school tuition. Instead of going to a private academy, however, Minnie took a state examination for a teaching certificate at age sixteen. Passing the test, she took a job teaching at a community school near New Waverly.

After teaching school for a year, Minnie decided that the classroom was not her true calling, so she enrolled at the University of Texas Medical Branch in Galveston to study pharmacy. Her studies were interrupted by a devastating hurricane that hit Galveston and killed more than 5,000 people, making it the deadliest storm in American history. Minnie helped the Red Cross (including the organization's founder, Clara Barton) procure funds and donations of clothing and food to assist displaced residents. After receiving her degree the following year, Minnie took the Huntsville pharmacy job that she would quit because of pay disparity.

About a year after moving back to Huntsville, at age twenty, Minnie married Beverly Jean "Bill" Cunningham, a Huntsville lawyer and insurance executive. According to Minnie, Bill was "the best-looking man I ever saw." Like most wives of the era, Minnie did not work at a job, but she spent time volunteering in the community. In 1904 she helped Bill with his campaign for county attorney, which he won. It was Minnie's first experience with hands-on politics and was the catalyst for her entrance into the political arena.

In 1907 the couple moved to Galveston, where Bill had taken a new job with an insurance company. The city was still recovering from the hurricane damage, and Minnie got involved in the rebuilding effort. She joined the Women's Health Protective Association, which focused on reburying the bodies whose graves had been flooded. While in Galveston, the couple adopted two children, though little is known about them.

As the years passed, Minnie continued to work for progressive causes, especially women's suffrage. The more involved she became in public affairs, however, the more her marriage suffered—Bill would have preferred a more traditional wife. Even more damaging to the relationship was Bill's alcoholism. Nevertheless, they managed to keep the marriage intact.

In 1910 Minnie was elected president of the Galveston Equal Suffrage Association. This position required that she tour the state to speak on the issue, putting more strain on the marriage. Five years later, she was elected president of the Texas Woman Suffrage Association (later called the Texas Equal Suffrage Association). Minnie was a strong leader and a powerful and persuasive speaker. During her first year in office, the number of local auxiliaries to the association quadrupled. She remained president for three more terms.

In her position as president of the TESA, Minnie felt she could accomplish more if she moved nearer to the seat of power in Austin. She moved to the Texas capital in 1917 and set up business near the statehouse. America had just entered World War I, the "War to End All Wars," and the shrewd Minnie saw a way to use the nation's wartime mood to win support for her cause. The suffragettes sold war bonds and helped the Red Cross in its many projects, actions that would prove women's value to the nation. The suffragists also pointed out the hypocrisy of a country that was fighting for democracy while denying half its own population the right to vote.

In the meantime, Minnie and some of her associates were also pursuing another cause. In anticipation of America's entrance into World War I, the military had established a number of training bases in Texas. These bases were becoming overrun with drunkenness, gambling, and prostitution. Like most women of the era, Minnie deplored such seedy activities. Although there were laws on the books against such shenanigans, city officials seldom enforced them. Gathering her supporters in San Antonio in June 1917, Minnie helped form the Texas Women's Anti-Vice Committee to patrol roadhouses and red-light districts around the military installations in El Paso, Fort Worth, Houston, and San Antonio. Every transgression they found was laid at the feet of city officials. Her cleanup efforts found enthusiastic support among local women and attracted more followers for the suffrage movement.

Minnie's hard work finally bore fruit in 1918, when Texas became the first southern state to pass a women's suffrage act. The victory attracted the attention of Carrie Chapman Catt, president of the National American Woman Suffrage Association, who persuaded Minnie to come to Washington and lobby Congress to pass a constitutional amendment for nationwide female suffrage. The following year, in a special session, Congress passed the Nineteenth Amendment to the Constitution, guaranteeing voting rights for women in every state, and sent it to the states for ratification. Minnie contacted governors all over the West and urged them to sign on. The amendment was ratified in August 1920.

With the taste of triumph on her lips, Minnie helped organize the National League of Women Voters (NLWV) in 1919, serving as executive secretary. Her speech at the NLWV's second annual convention apparently left quite an impression—twenty years later, first lady Eleanor Roosevelt remembered it, saying that it made her feel "that you had no right to be a slacker as a citizen, you had no right not to take an active part in what was happening to your country as a whole."

In 1927, after twenty-five years of marriage, Bill died. Minnie returned to Texas to settle the estate, but she did not immediately go back to Washington afterward. Instead, she chose to enter

Minnie Fisher Cunningham (right) poses with two unidentified supporters during her campaign for the U.S. Senate, 1928. —Courtesy Austin History Center, Austin Public Library

national politics by running for the United States Senate, becoming the first woman in Texas to do so. The incumbent was Earle B. Mayfield, a member of the Ku Klux Klan. Minnie's campaign platform included not only civil rights but also alcohol prohibition, tax reform, and support of the League of Nations (the precursor to the United Nations). Badly defeated in the Democratic primary, she threw her support to Thomas T. Connally, who beat Mayfield in the runoff and went on to win the general election.

Financially unstable after her husband's death, Minnie remained in Texas and took a paying job with Texas A&M University's extension service at College Station. Nine years later, she returned to

Washington to work for the Women's Division of the Agricultural Adjustment Administration (AAA) as an information specialist. The AAA, one of President Franklin Roosevelt's New Deal programs, helped raise farmers' income by limiting the amount of crops they could grow, thus keeping prices up. It was President Roosevelt who gave Minnie the nickname she relished and carried the rest of her life—Minnie Fish.

After resigning from the AAA in 1943, Minnie returned to Austin, where she took a keen interest in both Roosevelt's reelection campaign and the Texas gubernatorial race. When writer J. Frank Dobie declined to run for governor against incumbent Coke Stevenson, Minnie decided to run herself. Stevenson won the election, but Minnie made a surprisingly good showing for a female candidate, finishing second out of nine contenders.

In 1946, at age sixty-four, Minnie retired to her family's New Waverly farm to raise cattle and grow pecans. Although removed from the hustle of politics, she continued supporting liberal causes and Democratic candidates. In the 1950s she organized the Democrats of Texas, which catered to progressive ideals, and she was a driving force in the founding of the *Texas Observer*, a biweekly political magazine now published by the Texas Democracy Foundation. When the U.S. Supreme Court issued its 1954 ruling on *Brown v. Board of Education*, disallowing racial segregation in public schools, Minnie worked to implement desegregation in the schools of New Waverly.

Minnie had lost her fair share of elections, both as a supporter and a candidate, but she never gave up trying. In 1952 Minnie hit the campaign trail for Democratic presidential candidate Adlai Stevenson, who lost big to Dwight Eisenhower. She also worked on the campaign of Democrat Ralph Yarborough, who lost his 1954 bid for the Texas governorship. She did pick a winner, however, in 1960, when she set up the Democratic campaign headquarters in her hometown to support the John F. Kennedy and Lyndon Johnson ticket. By this time Minnie was in financial straits, having invested in so many political projects. She was pressed to sell off parts of Fisher farms piece by piece, ultimately shrinking it from 1,200 acres to less than 500 acres.

In 1964 Minnie fell and broke her hip, a serious injury that often leads to fatal complications such as congestive heart failure. On December 9, 1964, Minnie Fisher Cunningham passed away from heart disease at age eighty-two. She was interred in Hardy Cemetery in New Waverly. A state historical marker stands at the site of her family farm on State Highway 75.

Jovita Idar, date unknown —Courtesy Institute of Texas Cultures, University of Texas at San Antonio (084-0596), from collection of A. Ike Idar

7

Jovita Idar

"HEROINE OF LA RAZA"

On an April day in 1914, Jovita Idar stood alone before a group of angry Texas Rangers, blocking the doorway to the offices of *El Progreso*, a radical Spanish-language newspaper in Laredo. The twenty-eight-year-old journalist was trying to stop the men from shutting the paper down in response to articles denouncing Woodrow Wilson's order to send United States troops to the border. Outraged by the paper's criticism of the president, the Rangers set out to destroy the presses of *El Progreso*. The defiant Jovita stood her ground, countering that freedom of the press was guaranteed in the United States Constitution. Her fortitude that day caused the vigilantes to turn around. The next night, however, when the building was empty, the Rangers returned with sledgehammers and smashed the paper's printing press to pieces. This may have been the end of *El Progreso*, but Jovita Idar's fight was just getting started.

Jovita's courageous work as a journalist and activist exposed the racism and inequities faced by Mexican Americans in Texas in the early twentieth century. She also worked tirelessly in Texas communities as an educator, organizer, volunteer, speaker, and civil rights leader. As president of the feminist organization *La Liga Femenil Mexicanista* (the League of Mexican Women), Jovita oversaw programs to educate the poor children of Laredo. Later, she operated a free kindergarten for Mexican American youngsters.

Jovita Idar was born in Laredo, Texas, on September 7, 1885. She was the second of eight children born to Nicasio and Jovita Idar. Nicasio, a journalist, later operated a weekly Spanish-language newspaper, *La Crónica* (the *Chronicle*), which he took over in 1910. He idolized Abraham Lincoln and believed in equality for all Americans. The paper exposed the injustices Mexican Americans faced at the time, including school segregation, social and job discrimination, and even lynchings. *La Crónica* was the forerunner of the Chicano civil-rights publications that took root half a century later.

Before becoming a writer at her father's newspaper, Jovita was a teacher. In 1903, at age eighteen, she earned a teaching certificate from the Holding Institute in Laredo. She taught in the little hamlet of Los Ojuelos (today a virtual ghost town), about thirty miles southeast of Laredo. As a teacher Jovita faced challenging conditions. The school never had enough desks, books, or even writing materials for the students. In the winter, the school building was cold and dank. As much as she tried, Jovita could not persuade the Anglo (white) authorities to increase funding for the school, whose students were predominantly the children of Tejanos (Texans of Mexican descent).

In 1910 Jovita resigned her teaching position in frustration and went to work for *La Crónica*. Two of her brothers, Clemente and Eduardo, already worked there alongside their father. *La Crónica* was critical of Mexican-Anglo relations in Texas and throughout the United States, and of the discrimination Tejanos suffered in just about every facet of life. The paper called for equal treatment of Mexican Americans in the schools, the workplace, and the justice system. The newspaper also supported the rebellion in Mexico against the dictatorial president Porfirio Díaz.

Usually writing under the pseudonym A.V. Negra, Jovita focused on the plight of Mexican Americans and Mexican immigrants in Texas, especially along the border. She particularly railed against the violent acts of the Texas Rangers, *Los Rinches*, who regularly and without consequences harassed, terrorized, and murdered Tejanos. The number of Mexican Americans lynched by the Rangers has been estimated in the thousands. One of the incidents Jovita reported on involved a fourteen-year-old Laredo boy accused of and arrested for murder. Before a trial could be convened, an Anglo mob broke into the jail, hauled him outside, and beat him to death. The vigilantes then tied his body to a buggy and dragged it through the streets of Laredo.

Another atrocity was the case of Antonio Rodríguez, a young ranch hand in Rocksprings. On November 2, 1910, the wife of a white rancher was raped and murdered in her home. Rodríguez, who confessed to the crime, was arrested and jailed the following day. The prisoner's confession may or may not have been coerced. The next day, a mob of some fifty men broke into the jail, dragged Rodríguez off, tied him to a tree, and burned him alive. Jovita reported, "The crowd cheered when the flames engulfed his contorted body. They did not even turn away at the smell of his burning flesh and I wondered if they even knew his name."

Whether or not Rodríguez was guilty, he was entitled to a trial, and the brutality of the vigilantes' actions were in no way justifiable. Yet such sadistic occurrences were commonplace. When it came to Tejanos, laws protecting accused prisoners—and citizens in general—were rarely enforced.

The Rodríguez lynching sparked riots in Mexico, especially in the border towns. The Mexican government protested the horrific act and even demanded reparations, which the U.S. government refused, maintaining that Rodríguez was an American citizen, not a Mexican.

This issue and others were soon overshadowed by the onset of the Mexican Revolution on November 20, 1910. *La Crónica* supported the rebels, led by Francisco Madero, in their efforts to overthrow the regime of Porfirio Díaz, who had declared himself the winner of an obviously rigged election. Although Díaz was forced out less than a year later, subsequent presidents fared no better in implementing reforms, and the rebellion dragged on under various leaders for a decade.

Meanwhile, in September 1911, *La Crónica* organized a convention of Tejano political leaders, activists, journalists, and others to discuss the issues of the times on both sides of the border. Throngs of supporters gathered in Laredo for the meeting, called *El Primer Congreso Mexicanista* (the First Mexican Congress), to debate solutions to the educational, social, labor, and economic injustices faced by the Tejano community. Jovita encouraged women to attend the congress, and many did. For some of them, it was the first opportunity they'd ever had to be politically active.

A few weeks later, in October 1911, some of the women who attended the convention formed *La Liga Femenil Mexicanista*, with Jovita serving as its first president. Under the motto *"Por la raza y para la raza"* (of the people and for the people), the group established programs to educate the poor children of Laredo. The women soon expanded La Liga's mission to include collecting food, clothing, and school supplies for those unable to afford such necessities. The organization also began conducting study sessions to help women educate themselves. *La Crónica* published the agendas of the meetings, fundraiser announcements, and updates of La Liga's activities.

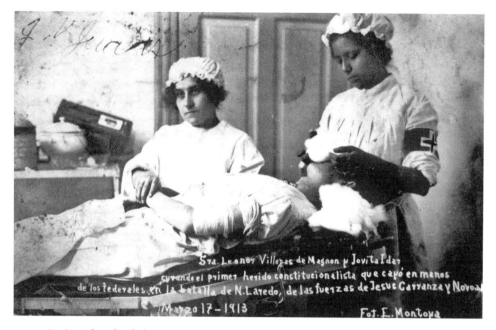

Jovita Idar (right) and Leonor Villegas de Magnon at work as White Cross nurses, 1913 —Courtesy Institute of Texas Cultures, University of Texas at San Antonio (084-0597), from collection of A. Ike Idar

As Jovita performed her good works in Texas, the Mexican Revolution continued to rage south of the border. In March 1913, the war came to the U.S.–Mexico border on the Rio Grande with a battle in Nuevo Laredo, Mexico, across the river from Laredo. Jovita and her friend Leonor Villegas de Magnon, along with some other Laredo women, crossed the Rio Grande to help the wounded Mexican rebels. With bullets flying all around them, the women located the wounded, administered first aid, moved them to hospitals, and assisted the doctors. Putting their own lives on the line, these volunteer nurses saved hundreds of men.

Shortly after the battle, Jovita helped Leonor found *La Cruz Blanca* (the White Cross), a group similar to the Red Cross, to organize nursing efforts. As the rebel forces moved across northern Mexico, La Cruz Blanca followed. Jovita risked her life as a White Cross nurse for months before going back to Laredo. Upon her return home in late 1913, Jovita went to work for another newspaper, *El Progreso*, where she spoke out against the policies of President Woodrow Wilson.

Immediately after taking office in January 1913, Wilson had denounced the revolution in Mexico, resulting in violence between Mexican rebels and Americans along the border. In response, the president sent federal troops to Texas and Arizona. Jovita and *El Progreso* vehemently opposed Wilson's actions and published many articles and editorials condemning them. Taking the criticism as an affront to federal (i.e., white) authority, the Texas Rangers went to Laredo to destroy the paper, which, in spite of Jovita's bold resistance, they did.

Unable to resurrect *El Progreso*, Jovita returned to her father's newspaper, *La Crónica*. Only a few weeks later, on July 17, 1914, Jovita's father, Nicasio, died. Jovita took over operation of *La Crónica* for a while, but within a couple of years she closed the paper down. In 1916 she and her brothers founded another weekly paper, *Evolución*, in Laredo.

In May 1917, Jovita married a local plumber and craftsman, Bartolo Juárez. Shortly afterward, the couple moved to San Antonio, where Jovita again became politically active. Along with Bartolo she formed *El Club Demócrata*, a Hispanic branch of the Democratic Party. She also served as an interpreter for Spanish-speaking patients in a county hospital and established a free bilingual kindergarten for Tejano children. Later in life she became editor of *El Heraldo Cristiano* (the *Christian Herald*), a publication of the Methodist Church in San Antonio.

Jovita Idar Juárez died in San Antonio on June 15, 1946, at age sixty, of an unidentified illness. She and Bartolo had no children. Bartolo Juárez died in 1958.

Jovita is remembered as the "Heroine of La Raza." She appears in the University of Texas at Austin's Gallery of Great Texas Women, and she is one of fifteen Latinas to be honored by the National Women's History Project. Her best-known quote appears on the "Wall of Words" at the Women's Museum in Washington, D.C.: "Educate a woman and you educate a family."

Bessie Coleman as a young woman, date unknown —Courtesy
National Air and Space Museum, Smithsonian Institution

8

Bessie Coleman

"BRAVE BESSIE"

On June 15, 1921, Bessie Coleman, age twenty-nine, became the first black woman to earn a pilot license. She did not receive her license from her home state of Texas, however, or even from her home country. In her day, both women and people of color had limited civil rights in America, so aviation schools legally could—and did—reject applications on the basis of race and/or sex. Being both black and female, Bessie had no chance to train in the United States. She had to travel to France—a more progressive country—to accomplish her lifelong ambition to fly.

Elizabeth "Bessie" Coleman was born on January 26, 1892, in a primitive one-room cabin in Atlanta, Texas, near the Arkansas state line. She was the tenth of thirteen children (four of whom died in infancy). When Bessie was two years old, the family moved about two hundred miles west to Waxahachie, where Bessie's father, George, sharecropped on a small piece of land outside of town and built a three-room house for his large family.

Waxahachie was in Ellis County, one of the busiest cotton-producing regions in the country. To help support the family, the children worked in the cotton fields when they were old enough. Picking cotton in the hot sun with a large bag strapped to her back, Bessie vowed to herself that this would not be her future.

Bessie's mother, Susan, raised the children by herself after George left the family and moved to Indian Territory (Oklahoma) in 1901. Three-quarters Indian, George believed he would have a better life on a reservation. Susan, however, having no desire to live on an Indian reservation, stayed in Texas with the children. Some of Bessie's siblings were grown and had left home by then, but the younger children, including Bessie, pitched in to help the family survive. During the day, Susan worked as a housekeeper in the home of a white family, leaving Bessie to care for her younger sisters. In the evenings the girls helped their mother with the washing and ironing she took in to help make ends meet. When the chores were done, Bessie loved to read to her three little sisters, Nilus, Georgia, and Elois.

Bessie was an avid reader and gifted in math. Dedicated to getting an education, she walked four miles each way to attend a ramshackle, one-room "colored" school. Following her graduation from high school at age seventeen, she entered the Colored Agricultural and Normal (teaching) University (today's Langston University) in Langston, Oklahoma, but she ran out of money and had to leave school after only one semester. When she returned home, she supported herself as a laundress.

Railroad porters passing through Waxahachie often brought newspapers into town, and Bessie would sometimes get a copy of the black-owned *Chicago Defender*. According to the paper's editor, Chicago was a city where African Americans could find a decent-paying job among their own people. Bessie's older brother, Walter, had moved there years earlier and found work as a porter. In 1915 Bessie joined Walter in the Windy City, where she enrolled in beauty school, then got a job as a manicurist in a downtown barbershop. Some sources claim that Bessie got married in Chicago, in July 1917, but she kept the marriage a secret and never used her husband's name. The two soon separated.

By this time, World War I was under way, and Bessie's brothers, Walter and John, had joined the war effort, serving in the all-black Eighth Army National Guard. Around this time, people began talking about a new type of equipment the military was now using—the airplane. In the barbershop where she worked, Bessie listened to the stories of returning veterans. They spoke of Europe, where black people had the same rights as whites. They spoke of the battles they had fought in their segregated regiments. And some of them spoke of the newfangled flying machines, although "Negro" Americans were not allowed to pilot them.

Women were not allowed to fly in the military, either, although there were a few American women who were licensed pilots, such as Harriet Quimby, Ruth Law, Elinor Smith, and the Stinson sisters. But in early-twentieth-century America, women who took part in male-dominated activities were widely frowned upon. Flying was one of these activities. Most male pilots felt that women did not have the physical, mental, or emotional capacity to do the job. Someday, Bessie Coleman would join the sisterhood of aviators who proved them wrong.

When John returned home after the war, he began singing the praises of the French, who believed in both racial equality and gender equality. In France, he said, there was no racism, and women had careers. French women even flew planes! One evening, after Bessie told him about her desire to learn to fly, John, slightly drunk, mocked her ambition. She was just a poor colored girl, he said scornfully. She could never fly like those French women. Then and there, Bessie Coleman decided to become a pilot.

To save up some money, Bessie took a better-paying job managing a chili restaurant on Chicago's South Side. In the meantime, she also shared her dream with several prominent black Chicagoans, hoping to secure financial support for her trip to France. One of those who encouraged and partially financed Bessie's quest was *Chicago Defender* editor Robert S. Abbott. Abbott knew that if Bessie succeeded, her achievement would inspire the black community and, in the process, boost readership for his newspaper.

In November 1920, Bessie set sail for Europe. She was rejected at the first school to which she applied, but she was accepted at the renowned École d'Aviation des Frères Caudron at Le Crotoy, north of Paris. While training there she witnessed the death of a fellow student. Nevertheless, she stood firm—she was going to become a pilot. As she said later, "The sky is the only place where there is no prejudice, the only place to be free."

In 1921 the Fédération Aéronautique Internationale issued Bessie Coleman an international pilot license. She returned to the United States with ambitious plans in mind. First off, she was determined to make a career of flying. Second, she wanted to buy her own plane. In addition, she envisioned opening a flying school for African Americans. But she would need money.

In the 1920s, before commercial flying took hold, pilots, mostly from the war, found work in the entertainment industry. Barnstorming shows, or flying circuses, were popular forms of entertainment. But Bessie found that she did not have enough training to perform the daredevil tricks the industry demanded. In February 1922 she went back to Europe for more flying lessons, returning to the United States a few months later.

Back in America, Bessie made arrangements to perform in several air shows, which she promoted by promoting herself. Beautiful, dramatic, and articulate, she created an image of herself as an exciting new breed of aviator—bold, daring, and confident, yet still feminine. Her first major exhibition took place on September 3, 1922, at New York's Curtis Field. She was billed as "the world's greatest woman flyer." The show was a huge success, which encouraged her to keep going. Later that year she performed before a home crowd at Chicago's Checkerboard Airdrome (now Midway

Bessie in her flying gear, date unknown —Courtesy
National Air and Space Museum, Smithsonian Institution

Airport). Her friend Robert Abbott made sure the *Defender* gave her much publicity, dubbing her "Queen Bess."

The most breathtaking stunt in the show was actually an accident, one that could have proved fatal. Flying in a figure eight to honor Chicago's Eighth Regiment, the unit her brother served in during the war, Bessie dove into a free fall at the top of the loop. The only restraints she had in the open cockpit were a seatbelt and centrifugal force. On the way down, her plane stalled. It was only by luck that the engine kicked in again at the last second, preventing a deadly crash.

Shortly after her first season of air shows, Bessie was offered a movie role, but in the end she turned it down because her character was depicted as a hapless black stereotype. Because the film's producer, the Seminole Film Producing Company, was a black-operated business, Bessie's rejection of the project alienated many African Americans. She was labeled as haughty, temperamental, and eccentric. And the antagonism went beyond the film industry. Black men resented her for doing something they couldn't, and black women found her flamboyant behavior inappropriate and embarrassing.

Undaunted, Bessie spent the next several years putting on shows throughout the country, thrilling audiences and regaining her popularity. Her flying feats were so daring that she picked up the nickname "Brave Bessie."

In early 1923 she bought her first plane, an army surplus JN4, or "Jenny." Unfortunately, only a few days later, Bessie was flying to a show when the plane went into a stall at three hundred feet and crashed. The accident destroyed the Jenny and knocked Bessie unconscious. Suffering a broken leg, cracked ribs, and lacerations to her face, she was in the hospital for three months. It took her almost a year to fully recuperate.

As soon as she recovered, she went back on the air-show circuit, and by 1925 she had saved enough for a down payment on another surplus Jenny. By this time she had moved back to Texas, establishing a headquarters in Houston. During those years, while continuing to fly in exhibitions, Bessie began to go on speaking tours in which she hoped to get people of color interested in aviation. Appearing at churches, schools, and theaters, she enthralled audiences with tales of her exploits in the wild blue yonder.

Bessie was devoted to the cause of helping her fellow African Americans. In Houston, she once took the city's black residents— at least those who dared—on a free bird's-eye tour. The local black newspaper, the *Houston Informer*, proudly noted that it was "the first time the colored public of the South had been given the opportunity to fly."

Using her popularity and fame, Bessie challenged the segregation rules of the era. She refused to perform unless black folks were allowed to attend the show, and she insisted that they enter through the same gate as whites. One time in Orlando, Florida, she demanded that planes fly over the city's black neighborhoods and drop invitations to her show.

In Orlando, Bessie met a millionaire, Edwin M. Beeman, heir to the Beeman Chewing Gum fortune. He had long had an interest in flying and gave Bessie the money to pay off the balance due on her Jenny. But the plane, a leftover from World War I, needed some work. A mechanic in Dallas, William Wills, agreed to fix up the Jenny and fly it to Jacksonville, Florida, where Bessie was scheduled to perform. En route, Wills had to make three emergency landings for repairs. Some pilots who saw the plane land in Jacksonville said that the craft was so worn out they couldn't believe it had made it all the way from Dallas.

The exhibition in Jacksonville, sponsored by the Negro Welfare League, was scheduled for May 1, 1926. Bessie, who had recently added skydiving to her performances, had agreed to do a parachute jump. The day before the show, April 30, Bessie was conducting a test flight to determine a good spot for her jump. She was riding in the passenger seat so she could check the field, while Wills had the controls. Because she needed unrestricted movement to be able to lean out of the plane to see below, Bessie was wearing neither a seatbelt nor a parachute. They had been in the air for about twelve minutes when they ran into trouble.

At about 500 feet (estimates vary up to 1,500 feet), the Jenny suddenly went into a nosedive then flipped upside down, dropping Bessie to her death. Wills went down with the plane and died on impact.

Bessie was only thirty-four years old when she died. Her plane was so badly damaged that officials could not determine the cause of the crash. It is believed that a lost wrench may have jammed the controls.

Memorials were held in Jacksonville and Orlando before Bessie's body was transported by train to Chicago, where thousands of admirers attended her funeral. She was interred in Chicago's Lincoln Cemetery. Although Bessie never had a chance to open her flying school, her friend and fellow black pilot William J. Powell established the Bessie Coleman Aero Club in Los Angeles in 1930. More African American flight schools soon followed.

Many other tributes to Bessie came after her death. The city of Chicago recognized Bessie in 1990 when Mayor Richard M. Daley renamed a street for her. In 1995 the United States Postal Service issued a commemorative stamp in her honor. The same year, Bessie was inducted into the Women in Aviation Hall of Fame, and in 2000, into the Texas Aviation Hall of Fame. Each year on the anniversary of her death, African American pilots fly low over Lincoln Cemetery and drop flowers on her grave.

Colonel Oveta Hobby, Women's Army Corps —Courtesy
Woodson Research Center, Fondren Library, Rice University

9

Oveta Culp Hobby

SHE DID IT ALL

In her lifetime, Oveta Culp Hobby earned so many honors that there is no room to list them all here. She was the first Secretary of the Department of Health, Education, and Welfare (and the second woman ever to become a member of a president's cabinet); the organizer and first commander of the Women's Army Corps (WAC); a Texas state legislative parliamentarian; and an inductee in the Texas Women's Hall of Fame. She appeared on the cover of *Time* magazine twice. But these accomplishments hardly scratch the surface.

Oveta Culp was born on January 19, 1905, in Killeen, Texas, about fifty miles north of Austin. She was the second of seven children born to Isaac (Ike) and Emma Culp. Her mother christened her Oveta after a character in a romance novel, the name supposedly an American Indian word for "forget." Oveta Culp, however, was hardly forgetful. She had a sharp and focused mind and a will of iron.

Being involved in public affairs and public service came naturally to Oveta. Ike was a state legislator and a lawyer. Emma collected clothing, food, and money for the less fortunate, and one of Oveta's duties as a young girl was to deliver care baskets to people going through hard times in her community.

Even at a very young age, Oveta was an independent thinker. When she was a child, in the early 1900s, a big issue of the day was alcohol abuse. Once in Sunday school, the children were asked to sign a pledge that they would never drink. Oveta shocked everyone when she refused to sign. Although at age five, she had no inclination to drink liquor, the precocious Oveta figured that she might want to do so someday, and she did not want to give her word unless she was sure she could keep it.

In elementary school, Oveta made it a daily routine to stop by her father's office on her way home from school and listen to the men talk law and politics. She even began perusing the books in her father's vast library, reading at a level far beyond her years. By age ten, she was reading the *Congressional Record*, and by thirteen she had read the Bible three times.

Another story about the bold and brainy young Oveta involved a spelling contest she entered in the sixth grade. The prize was a Bible. As described in a *Time* magazine article published years later, "In a firm, quiet voice [Oveta] told the teacher she might as well go right ahead and inscribe the Bible . . . to Oveta Culp." Oveta wasn't being haughty; she simply knew she was the best speller and that her victory was inevitable.

After Oveta's father was elected to the state legislature in 1919, he often took his fourteen-year-old daughter to Austin with him. Sitting beside her father in the statehouse, Oveta listened enraptured to each session of the legislature. Neither she nor her father gave much thought to the amount of school she was missing. In spite of the frequent absences, she graduated near the top of her class at Temple High School.

There were few fields that the young Oveta could not conquer. In high school, one of her concentrations was dramatic speaking (which was then called elocution). One speech she gave was so effective that she was offered a contract to tour with Chautauqua, a renowned traveling adult-education program of the era. She was disappointed when her parents refused to let her go. Undaunted, she turned her talents in another direction, forming the "Jolly Entertainers," a group of teenage musicians who performed at charitable benefits to raise money for local churches.

Upon graduating high school, Oveta spent two years at the University of Mary Hardin-Baylor in Belton, Texas. While still a student, she took a job as a cub reporter for the *Austin Statesman*. In 1925, while working toward her law degree at the University of Texas School of Law, the twenty-year-old Oveta was asked to serve as the state's legislative parliamentarian, a person who ensured that the legislators abided by the rules of order. She held this position until 1931. She later wrote a book on parliamentary procedures in

Parliamentarian Oveta Culp stands with her fellow government officials at the Capitol in Austin, circa 1930 —Courtesy Texas State Library and Archives Commission

the Texas legislature, entitled *Mr. Chairman*. In 1938 the book was introduced as a textbook in the Texas public school system.

While still working as parliamentarian in the Capitol, Oveta became clerk of the State Banking Commission, where she codified Texas banking laws. After that she served as clerk for the legislature's judicial committee. She also became secretary of the Texas Democratic Club. In 1928 she helped develop plans for the Democratic National Convention, which was to be held in Houston.

Her talents and energy put her in constant demand. She was asked to work on many campaigns, including Thomas Connally's bid for United States Senate, which he won, and Walter E. Monteith's run for mayor of Houston, which was also successful. Upon becoming mayor, Monteith offered Oveta the position of assistant to the city attorney, which she accepted with the provision that she would be allowed to return to Austin to continue as parliamentarian when the legislature convened. That same year, 1930, Oveta made her first and only bid for public office, as a candidate for the state legislature. Her opponent, who was supported by the Ku Klux Klan, accused Oveta of being a radical. After she lost, she never ran for office again, instead focusing on other ways to serve the public.

While in Houston, Oveta renewed an old acquaintance with William Pettus Hobby, a longtime friend of her father and former governor of Texas. Hobby, who was also a newspaper publisher, had come to Houston in 1924, a few years after his term as governor was over, to oversee the *Houston Post-Dispatch*. His first wife, Willie, died in 1929, not long before he became reacquainted with Oveta.

William Hobby had become governor in 1917. He was serving as lieutenant governor under James Ferguson when the latter, about to be impeached, resigned. As the next in line, Hobby assumed the governorship. In spite of his impeachment, Ferguson ran for governor again in 1918, but he lost in the primary to Hobby, who defeated him by the largest majority ever seen in a Democratic primary. Hobby was a popular governor who supported education and energy conservation.

Will Hobby was much older than Oveta, but the two proved to be soul mates. They were married on February 23, 1931, when she was twenty-six and he was fifty-three. They would be together for the next thirty-three years. Soon after their wedding, Oveta took a job with Will's newspaper, where she reviewed books, edited copy, wrote editorials, and assisted her husband, the paper's editor and publisher. In 1939 the Hobbys purchased the paper, renamed the *Houston Post*, which Will ran successfully for the next twenty-five years.

In 1932, on her own birthday, Oveta gave birth to William Pettus Hobby Jr., who later went by "Bill." When he grew up, Bill, like his father, served as lieutenant governor of Texas. Exactly five years after Bill was born—again on Oveta's birthday—Jessica Hobby came into the world. Though Oveta was devoted to her children, motherhood did not slow her down. While still working at the newspaper, she became involved in a number of arts and social-service organizations, including the Museum of Fine Arts, the Junior League, the Symphony Orchestra Committee, and the Mobilization for Human Needs. She also served as president of the Texas League of Women Voters.

In the summer of 1936, Oveta and her husband were in a serious accident when the engine of the private plane in which they were flying caught fire. Landing in a vacant field, the crew and passengers struggled to get free of the burning plane. Will was knocked unconscious in the crash, and Oveta pulled him from the wreckage. She then stepped forward to aid the pilot, who was badly burned. Borrowing a car from a local farmer, Oveta drove to the hospital with the injured victims and upon arrival assisted the doctor in preparing them for treatment. She was so calm that the doctor did not realize that Oveta had been in the accident herself. When he found out, he immediately had her admitted into the hospital with the others.

In June 1941, as World War II raged in Europe, Oveta was offered her biggest challenge yet. She was in Washington on business when U.S. Army General David Searles approached her and asked if she would be willing to organize a women's branch of the army. Though the women's army corps did not yet exist, nor had the United States yet entered the war, many government officials believed that war was imminent, and the military was trying to plan ahead. At first Oveta turned down General Searles's offer; between caring for her family, doing her job, and managing her other commitments, she had no time to take on a massive project. But she did agree to help with the plans by drafting an organizational chart for the War Department's newly formed Women's Activities Office and recommending ways women might be able to support the military.

The idea of a women's army corps was revolutionary. In those days, women could not serve in the armed forces except in the Army Nurse Corps. Earlier in 1941, Massachusetts Congresswoman Edith Nourse Rogers had introduced a bill to form a women's army corps, in which women could handle routine administrative and support duties in order to free more men for the front lines. The bill was not picked up in Congress, but some army brass, such as Searles, saw the sense in it and pursued the idea. Should the proposal be reintroduced, some plans would already be in place.

When Oveta finished drafting the chart for Searles, the general asked if she would come back to Washington to get the plans rolling. She initially said no, but when she told her husband of the offer he encouraged her to grab this opportunity to serve the country. Oveta took the job heading the Women's Interest Section of the War Department Bureau of Public Relations.

On December 7, 1941, Japan attacked Pearl Harbor, thrusting the United States into World War II. The overwhelming needs of the military prompted a revival of the idea of a women's army corps, and Edith Nourse Rogers's bill was reintroduced in Congress. To gather information in support of the bill, Secretary of War Henry Stimson and Army Chief of Staff George C. Marshall assigned Oveta the task of sorting out which jobs women could do in the army with the least amount of training. When the plans were complete, Oveta testified before Congress about her recommendations for the organization of a women's corps. Her congressional testimony impressed many people in and out of the political arena. The bill authorizing the formation of the Women's Auxiliary Army Corps (WAAC) was passed by Congress in May 1942 and signed into law by President Roosevelt.

The new program would need a director, so General Marshall naturally approached Oveta for her suggestions. When she presented him a list of candidates, Marshall glanced at it, laid it on his desk face down, looked at Oveta, and said, "I'd rather you took the job." Having already done more than she had signed on for, and aching to return home to her family, Oveta declined. Yet once again, Will convinced her to accept the position. She was given the rank of major.

Oveta did not realize how challenging the job would be until she started. As director, she was on the go constantly, promoting the corps, recruiting women, making arrangements for the enlistees, and most importantly, acting as a role model. She often worked into the night, going home only to shower before returning to her office for another day of work. Her pay for this demanding position? One dollar a year.

Making her job even more difficult, the army gave Oveta little support. In this day and age, it is hard to believe the resistance Oveta was up against in getting the WAAC up and running. When she asked the army engineers to design barracks for the WAAC volunteers, for example, they informed her that they did not work for the women's corps. It was up to Oveta and her staff to draw up plans for their barracks. Also, even though she was an officer, she was not given a vehicle; whenever she needed a ride, she had to call the motor pool. Some of the restrictions were downright petty— for instance, although she was allowed to use the facilities of the officers club, she had to enter through the back door. A woman of lesser ability and stamina would have thrown up her hands and walked away.

Did Oveta's efforts pay off? Considering the way things started, the WAAC made stunning progress. Initially, and reluctantly, Congress listed fifty-four fields in which women could work. By the end of Oveta's reign, the number had grown to 239. According to one commentator, the WAAC proved that women "could often do the work of two men in certain tasks—from secretarial work to PBX [telephone switchboard] operations to kitchen patrol to parachute folding." On January 17, 1944, Oveta appeared on the cover of *Time* magazine for the first time.

The formation of the WAAC had been a political compromise. Because many people in the military and in the general public opposed the idea of women serving in uniform, the WAAC was created as an auxiliary body, not part of the U.S. Army. This meant that WAAC enlistees did not receive full army pay, benefits, and protections. But when, under Oveta Hobby's direction, the WAAC proved such a success, many people began to feel the women's position in the auxiliary corps was unfair. Finally, in July 1943, Congress passed a bill authorizing the induction of women into the regular army. The WAAC became the Women's Army Corps (WAC), and the women in it were now full-fledged army personnel. With the establishment of the WAC, Oveta was given the rank of colonel.

Within a year after the establishment of the WAAC in May 1942, commanders from all theaters of action began requesting more women auxiliaries. By the end of 1944, the army had received requests for 600,000 female personnel, far exceeding the number of available recruits. At its peak in April 1945, the WAC comprised nearly 100,000 active servicewomen, of whom more than 16,000 were serving overseas.

In January 1945, Oveta was awarded the Distinguished Service Medal; she was the first woman ever to receive this high military honor. The citation read, in part, "without guidance or precedents in the United States military history to assist her, Colonel Hobby established sound policies. . . . Her contribution to the war effort of the nation has been of important significance."

Oveta's success in establishing the WAAC and later the WAC inspired the formation of the Navy WAVES (established as a full military reserve division in August 1942), the Coast Guard SPARS (established as a reserve division in November 1942), the Marine Corps Women's Reserve (established as a reserve unit in February 1943), and the Women Airforce Service Pilots (established as an auxiliary unit in August 1943). The WAC was dissolved in 1978; thereafter, women in the army served as regular soldiers in the same units as men.

Oveta had far exceeded her own ambitious goals, but she paid a price—by 1945 she was thoroughly exhausted. In July of that year, she resigned. Her husband whisked her off to a hospital in New York for a complete rest. When she arrived back in Houston, she was welcomed home with a huge banquet.

After she returned home from the army, Oveta, like many other veterans, returned to her civilian work. By now Will had acquired a radio station and a television station, the latter representing a brand-new technology. Oveta directed both stations and also resumed her public-service work, volunteering on many committees and boards, including those of the National Red Cross, the American Cancer Society, the Society of Newspaper Editors, and the American Assembly. In 1948 she went to Geneva, Switzerland, as a member of the U.S. delegation to the United Nations Conference on Freedom of Information and the Press. Later she served as president of the Southern Newspaper Publishers Association, and the University of Missouri School of Journalism awarded her an honors medal.

Shortly after the war, Oveta served as co-chair for the Armed Forces Day celebration in Houston. She ran into a strong difference of opinion with a man on the committee who wanted to ban black servicemen from the event. Her wartime experience had driven home the ideal of equal rights for all. She insisted that "No celebration of Armed Forces Day will be held in Houston which is not open to everyone who has served in our armed forces—regardless of race." A heated argument ensued, but with assistance from Will Hobby, Oveta shut the man down.

For his own part, Will was something of a crusader for equal rights. As editor of the *Houston Post*, he voiced opposition to Japanese detainment centers during the war, and later provided a forum for supporters of desegregation. In 1951 William and Oveta Hobby were recognized for distinguished service to the advancement of human relations by the National Conference of Christians and Jews.

Although they had been lifelong Democrats, in 1952 the Hobbys both backed Dwight Eisenhower for president, with Oveta working for the Democrats for Eisenhower in Texas. Soon after becoming president, Eisenhower appointed Oveta chair of the Federal Security Agency (FSA), a sub-cabinet-level office responsible for overseeing Social Security, food and drug safety, public health, and federal education funding. A few months later, in April 1953, the president created a new cabinet-level agency, the Department of Health, Education, and Welfare (HEW), to replace the FSA, and he named Oveta to head it. Oveta Hobby was the second woman ever to hold a federal cabinet post (the first was Frances Perkins, Secretary of Labor under President Franklin Roosevelt). A few weeks after her appointment as Secretary of HEW, on May 4, 1953, Oveta made her second appearance on the cover of *Time* magazine.

The most dramatic development during Oveta's tenure at HEW was Dr. Jonas Salk's creation of the polio vaccine. Polio is a serious infectious disease that causes paralysis in various parts of the body, including the lungs. It can be fatal, and those who survive are often left permanently disabled. Most victims are children, and there is no cure. The early twentieth century saw an increase in polio epidemics, terrifying the American public. Scientists worked for decades looking for a way to either cure or prevent this rampant killer. Finally, in 1952, medical researcher Dr. Jonas Salk developed a serum he believed would provide safe and effective protection against the dreaded disease.

As HEW Secretary, Oveta was responsible for deciding how to proceed with this desperately needed yet untested serum. Whether to release the vaccine before it had been thoroughly tested, or to hold back a substance that could save children's lives—either choice involved a serious risk to public health. Oveta decided to make the serum legally available on a voluntary basis. Fortunately the vaccine worked, and the government soon launched a program to inoculate children on a massive scale. Between 1953 and 1957, the annual number of polio cases fell from 35,000 to 5,600. By 1961, only 161 cases appeared. Today, polio is considered eradicated in most countries of the world.

This was not Oveta's only accomplishment as Secretary of HEW. Under her leadership, the department made improvements in food and drug laws, mental health services, nurse-training programs, and myriad other areas. Through HEW's Office of Education, Oveta spearheaded the building of more schools in anticipation of the postwar baby boom. She also secured funds for building hospitals, nursing homes, treatment centers, and many other medical facilities. Oveta headed HEW for thirty-one months. She might have remained longer had she not received bad news from home.

In 1955 William Hobby fell ill with severe bronchitis, and Oveta returned to Houston to care for him. At a press conference announcing her departure, President Eisenhower said to her, "None of us will forget your wise counsel, your calm confidence in the face of every kind of difficulty, your concern for people everywhere, the warm heart you brought to your job as well as your talent." One news service wrote, "Not since hundreds of people stood in Union Station and cheered Harry S. Truman . . . at the end of his term has anyone left office in Washington with such fanfare as was accorded Mrs. Hobby at the White House yesterday."

During her husband's nine-year struggle with chronic bronchitis, Oveta seldom left his side for more than a few hours at a time. Nevertheless, she resumed her position as president and editor of the *Houston Post*, and in 1956 she became chair of the board of directors of the Bank of Texas and the first female member of Mutual of New York's board of trustees. For Oveta, this was a light workload. She had many other offers, but she turned them down so she would have enough time for Will.

Oveta's husband never fully recovered from his respiratory problems. William P. Hobby died on June 7, 1964, at age eighty-six. A few years later, the Houston Municipal Airport was renamed William P. Hobby Airport in his honor.

After Will's death, Oveta took on more projects, serving on several public-service and government committees, including the president's National Advisory Commission on Selective Service and HEW's Vietnam Health Education Task Force. She remained phenomenally active for the rest of her life, serving on countless boards and committees.

The number of honors and awards Oveta Hobby received over her lifetime is staggering. She received honorary degrees from fifteen different colleges and universities. One of her most personally meaningful tributes came in December 1967, when the library at Central Texas College in Killeen, her hometown, was named for her. None other than the President of the United States, Lyndon Johnson, officiated at the dedication ceremony. In 1978 she became the first woman to be awarded the George Catlett Marshall Medal for Public Service by the Association of the United States Army. Another honor that must have made her especially proud was her induction into the Texas Women's Hall of Fame in 1984.

In addition to her own accomplishments, Oveta took pride in those of her children. She was in attendance when her son, William P. Hobby Jr., was inaugurated as lieutenant governor of Texas in 1975. Her daughter, Jessica, married diplomat Henry Catto and became a noted conservationist.

Oveta Culp Hobby died as a result of a stroke on August 16, 1995, at age ninety. She was interred beside her husband in Houston's Glenwood Cemetery.

Babe Didrikson Zaharias, circa 1930s
—Courtesy Babe Didrikson Zaharias Foundation

10

Babe Didrikson Zaharias

"BABE" OF BEAUMONT

In April 1953 pro golfer Mildred "Babe" Didrikson Zaharias underwent an operation for colon cancer. Her physicians said that she would never again play the game professionally. But the doctors did not understand the dynamo that was Babe. Fourteen weeks after her surgery, she was back on the golf circuit with the LPGA (Ladies Professional Golf Association).

The Golf Writers of America voted Babe the 1953 comeback player of the year. The following year, she won five tournaments, including the United States Open, and was awarded the Vare Trophy, an annual prize given to the LPGA golfer with the best scoring average. During her life, she also excelled at basketball, baseball, and many other sports, and she was an Olympic gold medalist in track and field. Not bad for a scraggly, working-class kid from southeast Texas.

Babe was born Mildred Ella Didriksen on June 26, 1911, in Port Arthur, Texas, near the Louisiana state line and about ninety miles east of Houston. She was the sixth of seven children born to Ole and Hannah Marie Didriksen. The family name was spelled Didriksen, in accordance with its Norwegian roots. However, school officials recorded Mildred's surname with an "o" rather than an "e," and she never bothered correcting it. Babe's parents had emigrated from Norway in the early 1900s. Ole was a carpenter by trade as well as a seaman. Hannah had been an expert ice skater and skier in the old country.

When Mildred was four years old, a hurricane struck the Port Arthur area and flooded the Didriksen home, so the family moved to Beaumont, about fifteen miles to the northwest. In Beaumont, Mildred's father built gymnastic equipment in the backyard of the family home, and he and Hannah encouraged all of their children to develop athletic skills. When she was young, Babe worked out with her sister, Lillie. Their brother Ole later played professional football for a while, and another brother, Arthur ("Bubba"), played three years of minor-league baseball. Lillie's twin, Louis, was a champion boxer in the Texas National Guard.

According to most sources, Babe acquired her nickname while playing sandlot baseball with neighborhood kids, who thought she batted like baseball idol Babe Ruth. Some members of her family, however, recalled that her mother and siblings called her "Baby," a pet name that stuck even after her younger brother, Bubba, was born.

According to another story about Babe as a young girl, she used to jump the neighbors' hedges as she ran down the street, as a kind of practice for her later hurdle jumping. To streamline the course, she wanted the height and width of the hedges to be even. When a hedge was larger than the others on the block, she would ask the homeowner to trim it down.

In high school, Babe was not a very good student. She was interested only in sports, and she played them all—baseball, basketball, golf, swimming, volleyball. The boys often taunted her, but she never backed down. Once, a heavily built football player at Babe's school laughingly challenged her to hit him on the chin. She swung once, knocking him out cold. Years later, the football player, Red Reynolds, bragged about being "dropped" by "the famous Babe Didrikson."

Her talents were not limited to athletics, however. She once won a high school typing contest, averaging eighty-six words a minute, a skill that would come in handy when she took her first job in an office. She also played the harmonica, sang, and tap-danced; some people believe that she could have been a professional performer. In fact, later in life, she did record a few songs with Mercury Records, the best-selling one being "I Felt a Little Teardrop," released in 1954. Adding to the extensive list of her talents, she was an expert seamstress and made many of her own clothes, including the outfits she wore on the golf course.

After watching Babe play in a basketball game in Houston during her senior year, Colonel M. J. McCombs recruited her to work for his company, Employers Casualty Company of Dallas, which sponsored a semiprofessional women's basketball team called the Golden Cyclones. During her two years at Employers Casualty, where she worked as an office clerk, she not only led the Golden Cyclones to a national championship but also inspired the company to expand its women's sports program to include track and field. It was in track that Babe would become a real star.

At the 1932 Amateur Athletics Union Championships, Babe placed in seven out of the eight track events she entered. Her performances, which broke four world records, qualified her for the 1932 Olympic Games in Los Angeles, where she again performed amazing feats. She participated in three events at the Olympics, breaking world records in all three and winning two gold medals (hurdles and javelin) and a silver (high jump). Babe's showing at the Olympics inspired more nicknames, including the "Texas Tornado," the "Terrific Tomboy," and "Whatta Gal." Babe's biographer May Kay Knief, however, maintains that her Olympic teammates hated her, finding her boastful and arrogant.

Back home in Texas, though, Babe received a well-deserved hero's welcome. According to Knief, "the police department band played

'Hail to the Chief'; she rode in the fire chief's open red limousine; there were roses and thrown confetti. The people loved her." To a country now in a deep depression, Babe brought a beam of light.

Babe became a darling of the press and was always available for interviews and photos. Grantland Rice, one of the finest sports writers of all time, was an unabashed Babe Didrikson fan. Of her Olympic performance he wrote: "She is beyond all belief until you see her perform. There you finally understand that you are look- ing at the most flawless section of muscle harmony, of complete mental and physical coordination the world has ever known. This may seem to be a wild statement, yet it happens to be 100 percent true. There is only one Babe Didrikson and there has never been another in her class—even close to her class."

Babe herself seemed to agree. Her statements to the press invari- ably showed boundless confidence. "I came out to beat everybody in sight and that's just what I'm going to do." In answer to a question about an upcoming track event, she replied, "Yep, I'm going to win the high jump Sunday and set a world record. I don't know who my opponents are and, anyways, it wouldn't make any difference."

Upon her return to Texas, Babe hoped to continue playing with the Golden Cyclones, but after her name appeared in an automobile ad, the AAU disqualified her from amateur athletics. Her family needed money, and Babe knew the value of her name, so for the next two years she promoted herself in a variety of ways. She pitched in a number of Major League Baseball spring-training games. She toured in a billiards road show. In basketball, she traveled with a woman's team called Babe Didrikson's All-Americans. Following that stint, she became a temporary member of an otherwise all- male, bearded baseball team called the House of David. She even appeared on the vaudeville stage, playing the harmonica and hitting plastic golf balls into the audience. Anything to make a buck.

In those days, women's sports were considered not only unimportant but, in some cases, downright unseemly. Athletics were thought to be a masculine purview, and many deemed sports an inappropriate activity for young ladies. In spite of her popularity following her Olympic wins, biographers William O. Johnson and Nancy P. Williamson noted, "her era was unsympathetic to women and, as a female athlete, she was seen by many as a freak. She was insulted, ignored, laughed at." Her tomboy style, cocky attitude, and involvement with male baseball teams did nothing to help her reputation, and many saw her as a poor role model for young women.

One of the few sports considered genteel enough for women was golf, more acceptable because of its association with the upper class. Babe decided to focus her efforts on becoming a championship golfer. In 1933 she moved to California to take lessons from Stan Kertes, a golf instructor of some renown. Babe practiced every day, eight to ten hours at a stretch, hitting as many as a thousand balls a day. After six months, she ran out of money and returned to Texas, but she continued to practice diligently. Although she lost her first amateur golf match, the Fort Worth Invitational in November 1934, Babe being Babe, she did not give up. The following spring, 1935, she won the Texas Women's Amateur Golf Championship before a crowd of hundreds.

Unfortunately, the Texas country-club set did not take kindly to seeing their socialite members upstaged by a working-class bumpkin. Ostensibly because she was not an amateur athlete (though she had never played golf professionally), the Texas Women's Golf Association managed to have Babe disqualified from playing in future amateur tournaments.

Making lemonade out of this sour development, Babe turned semipro, competing in open tournaments, playing in moneyed exhibition tours, and doing endorsements. She became a better and better golfer, thrilling spectators with her prowess. She could drive the ball 240 yards or more—as far as, if not farther than, many male golfers. "When I want to really blast one, I just loosen my girdle and let 'er fly," she quipped.

In 1938 Babe applied to enter the Professional Golf Association's Los Angeles Open, a major tournament played mostly by men, though the rules did not forbid women from entering. Sure enough, she got in, becoming the first woman ever to qualify for this tournament. She was teamed up with a minister and a pro wrestler named George Zaharias. Babe and George hit it off immediately, forming a friendship that soon blossomed into romance. Later that year, on December 23, 1938, they became husband and wife.

George Zaharias was born Theodore Vetoyanis in Pueblo, Colorado, on February 28, 1908. His family, who had emigrated from Tripoli, Greece, was so destitute that Babe's family seemed like millionaires by comparison. When he took up pro wrestling, he adopted the name George Zaharias, for a long-dead relative in Greece. In wrestling circles, George was known as "the Crying Greek from Cripple Creek." The "crying" part came from his shtick of shedding tears when he saw a fellow wrestler losing a bout. "Cripple Creek" was a reference to his Colorado birthplace, which was actually Pueblo, but Cripple Creek fit the rhyme.

Babe and George had a wonderful marriage for the first few years. George gave up wrestling to manage his wife's career. In 1943 Babe was reinstated as an amateur. She won seventeen consecutive golf titles, including the prestigious British Women's Open Amateur Championship; she was the first American ever to win it. It was at the British Open that the playful side of Babe's personality came out. Barefoot and wearing a kilt, she treated onlookers to a Texas version of the Highland fling.

In 1947 Babe and fellow female golfers Patty Berg and Betty Hicks helped found the Ladies Professional Golf Association

Babe and George Zaharias, circa 1940s
—Courtesy Babe Didrikson Zaharias Foundation

(LPGA). Babe was the LPGA's leading money winner between 1949 and 1951. In 1950 the Associated Press voted her Woman Athlete of the Half Century.

Meanwhile, Babe and George were having their ups and downs. Babe had at least one miscarriage, which pulled her into a deep depression. The couple tried to adopt a baby, but they were turned down because of their hectic, nomadic lifestyle. In 1949 they bought a golf course in the Forest Hills section of Tampa, Florida, moving into a large house overlooking the greens. Over the years, George, who'd always been a hefty man, put on even more weight, eventually tipping the scales at four hundred pounds. Babe joked about it, but later she, too, began to gain weight, and both of them were apparently drinking. It was clear that the two were growing apart. The press reported on their fighting and there were rumors of a pending divorce, but the couple never separated.

Babe was diagnosed with colon cancer in 1953. During her recovery, her good friend and fellow golfer Betty Dodd put her own career on hold to care for Babe. After her surgery, Babe went back on the golf circuit, often playing benefit tournaments for cancer research. She was the picture of hope and courage, a tribute to human tenacity.

Unfortunately, in June 1955 Babe learned that the cancer was back and had spread to her lymph nodes. She was admitted to a hospital in Galveston, but the doctors soon concluded that further treatment would be of no avail.

Babe spent the fifteen months she had left in and out of the hospital. Again, Betty Dodd spent a lot of time caring for her, while George seemed unwilling to help out much. Later, Babe's sister Lillie moved to Galveston to be near her. During Babe's last few months, she and George established the Babe Didrikson Zaharias Fund for a cancer clinic at the University of Texas Medical Branch.

Babe Didrikson Zaharias died at John Sealy Hospital in Galveston on September 27, 1956, at age forty-five. Her golf clubs were beside her, where she had kept them since entering the hospital. She was interred at Forest Lawn Memorial Park in Beaumont. Engraved on her tombstone is the motto, taken from a popular poem by Grantland Rice, "It's not whether you win or lose, it's how you play the game."

Babe's death created a cloud of sadness around the world, and she was remembered by none other than the president of the United States, Dwight Eisenhower: "She was a woman who, in her athletic career, certainly won the admiration of every person in the United States, all sports people over the world, and in her gallant fight against cancer, she put up one of the kind of fights that inspired us all. I think that every one of us feels sad that finally she had to lose this last one of all her battles."

After Babe's death, George returned to Florida. In 1962 he sold the golf course. Many years later, in 1981, he remarried. By then his health was failing and he was confined to a wheelchair. His second wife, Harriet, was, like George, from a Greek family in Pueblo, Colorado, and the two had known each other as children. Harriet cared for George until his death. George Zaharias passed away in Tampa on May 22, 1984, following a stroke.

Babe Zaharias left a stunning legacy not only as a world-class athlete, but also as a pioneer in promoting women's sports and defying female stereotypes. Among her countless accomplishments and honors, she was named Athlete of the Year by the Associated Press six times; was a four-time LPGA world champion; won the United States Women's Open three times and the Western Open four times; was named an All-American in basketball three times; was a double gold medalist at the 1932 Olympic Games; helped found the LPGA; was inducted into the World Golf Hall of Fame in 1951; and was the first winner of the Ben Hogan Trophy in 1953. In the last year of her life, she established the Babe Zaharias Trophy to honor outstanding female athletes and the Babe Didrikson Zaharias Fund for cancer research.

Even after her death, Babe received a number of posthumous honors. She won the USGA Bob Jones Award in 1957; was one of the first six inductees in the LPGA Hall of Fame in 1977; and was named Woman Athlete of the Twentieth Century by the Associated

Press in 1999. Today her name graces a number of places and organizations. After years of neglect, the golf course Babe and George had owned was taken over by the city of Tampa, which restored it to its former glory and reopened it in 1974; the Babe Zaharias Golf Course remains one of Florida's first-class golfing destinations. In 1999 the Babe and George Zaharias Golf Foundation was established in Tampa to help underprivileged children learn golf. And back in Texas, the Babe Didrikson Zaharias Park and Museum, dedicated to her life and career, opened in her hometown of Beaumont in 1976.

There will never be another Babe Didrikson Zaharias. But her life story has inspired thousands, if not millions, of female athletes who came after her, including 1970s tennis great Billie Jean King and 1980s and '90s Olympian Jackie Joyner-Kersee. Nearly single-handedly, she exploded the notion that female athletes were second-rate and opened the floodgates for women to make their marks in sports.

Babe may have been born a natural athlete, but she worked extraordinarily long and hard to make herself a great one. No one can say that Babe ever wasted an ounce of her talents.

BARBARA JORDAN
Houston

Barbara Jordan (detail), 62nd Texas Senate Session, 1971
—Courtesy State Preservation Board, Austin, Texas (CHA 1989.634)

11

Barbara Jordan

"VOICE OF GOD"

"You've got too much going against you. You're black, you're a woman, and you're large. People don't really like your image." That was the warning given to Barbara Jordan by one of her campaign advisers in 1962. Indeed, Barbara lost her bid for the Texas House of Representatives that year as well as in the following election of 1964. But Barbara Jordan did not give up.

By the time Barbara launched her third campaign in 1966, this time for a seat in the Texas Senate, several acts passed by Congress and upheld by the U.S. Supreme Court had helped level the playing field for minority voters and candidates. These included the 1964 Civil Rights Act; the 1964 ratification of the Twenty-fourth Amendment, which abolished poll taxes; and the 1965 Voting Rights Act. Thanks in large part to these legislative advances, Barbara won her bid for the Texas Senate, making her the first African American elected to the Texas Senate since the 1880s, and the first black woman in state history elected to that distinguished body.

Barbara Charline Jordan was born in Houston on February 21, 1936. She was the youngest of three daughters born to Benjamin Jordan, a Baptist minister, and Arlyne Jordan, who worked as a domestic servant. Barbara's father was a great influence on her. He taught her that race and poverty could not override intelligence and ability. With hard work and dedication, he assured his daughter, she could achieve her goals. Arlyne, too, taught Barbara important skills. As an orator in church, Arlyne believed in the power of the spoken word. Barbara's grandfather, John Ed Patten, reinforced Arlyne's lessons by reading to the girl from a pronunciation dictionary.

Barbara grew up in Houston's Fifth Ward, a predominantly black section of the city, where she attended Roberson Elementary School and Phyllis Wheatley High School. She was an active student, a member of her high school's honor society, and a winning debater. Barbara was inspired when a black female lawyer from Chicago, Edith Sampson, spoke at her high school for Career Day. Upon returning home that evening, Barbara announced that she was going to become a lawyer. Her mother was a bit skeptical, knowing that her daughter would be facing an uphill battle, especially in the South, but her idealistic father gave Barbara his full support.

After graduating in 1952 in the top five percent of her high school class, Barbara wanted to study political science at the University of Texas, but at that time, the university did not allow black students. Instead Barbara attended the predominantly black Texas Southern University (TSU) in Houston, where she pursued a double major in political science and history. At TSU she joined the Delta Sigma Theta sorority and became a national champion debater, defeating orators from such prestigious schools as Brown and Yale. She graduated magna cum laude ("with great distinction") in 1956.

Pursuing her goal of becoming a lawyer, Barbara attended Boston University School of Law, graduating in 1959. She passed the bar in both Massachusetts and Texas later that year. After teaching political science at Tuskegee Institute in Alabama for a year, she returned to Texas in 1960. Back in Houston, she established a law practice, which she ran out of her parents' home for the first three years. During the 1960 presidential election, Barbara helped campaign for John F. Kennedy and joined a movement to register black voters in Houston. These experiences provided her with her first taste of politics. Two years later, she was running for public office herself.

After her two unsuccessful bids for a seat in the Texas House of Representatives, Barbara was elected to the Texas Senate in 1966. With her eloquent but straightforward style and her knowledge of the law, she earned the respect of her thirty white, male colleagues. During one lengthy legislative session on March 21, 1967, the lieutenant governor chose Barbara to temporarily preside over the senate chamber, an action that broke another color barrier—she was the first African American ever to hold that responsibility. Continuing on her barrier-breaking path, she became the first African American to chair a major senate committee (Labor and Management Relations), and the first freshman senator, black or white, male or female, ever appointed to the Texas Legislative Council. Her colleagues named her Outstanding Freshman Senator.

It was also in 1967 that Barbara first met fellow Texan Lyndon B. Johnson, then president of the United States. Johnson had called her to Washington along with several other prominent civil-rights leaders to discuss upcoming legislation, the Fair Housing Act in particular. At the time, Barbara didn't realize that the president even knew her name. In a 1984 oral history, Barbara recalled that first meeting with Johnson: "He looked at my end of the table and he said 'Barbara, what do you think?' Well, I just . . . in the first place, I'm telling you, I didn't know the president knew me, and here he's looking down here saying 'Barbara' and then saying 'What do you think?'" Little did she know that the meeting would prove to be the beginning of a long relationship in which Johnson would serve as her mentor, political supporter, and friend until his death in January 1973.

Barbara served in the Texas senate for six years. In March 1972, during a special session of the Texas legislature, Senator Jordan was unanimously chosen president pro tempore, an honor never before bestowed upon an African American woman in any state. In this position, according to Texas tradition, she served as Governor for a Day on June 10, 1972, technically making her the first black female governor in U.S. history.

With so much success in the state legislature, Barbara was ready to try for national office. Running for the U.S. House of Representatives in 1972, Barbara beat her Republican rival in a landslide. Although she was not the first black woman to serve in the U.S. House—that honor went to Shirley Chisholm of New York, who

Barbara Jordan as president pro tempore of the Texas legislature, 1972 —Courtesy Texas State Library and Archives Commission

took office in 1969—Barbara Jordan was the first black woman ever elected to Congress from the South. She would go on to win two bids for reelection.

As the people's representative in Washington, Barbara sponsored bills to help the nation's poor, black, and disadvantaged citizens. For example, she sponsored a bill to expand the Voting Rights Act of 1965 to secure voting rights for Mexican Americans and other minorities and to outlaw certain unfair practices, such as literacy tests.

In 1973, just weeks before his death, former president Lyndon Johnson recommended Barbara for appointment to the House Judiciary Committee, and she served on this prominent committee during all three of her congressional terms. In her very first year on the committee, she found herself launched into the national spotlight. As a member of the Judiciary Committee, Barbara voted on the impeachment of President Richard Nixon after the infamous Watergate scandal. She voted "yes" for impeachment, making one of her most famous statements: "My faith in the Constitution is whole, it is complete, it is total. I am not going to sit here and be an idle spectator to the diminution, the subversion, the destruction of the Constitution."

Nixon's investigation was televised, beaming Barbara's face into the living rooms of mainstream America and making her a household name. Her perfect diction and booming voice (later called the "Voice of God") impressed both the public and her fellow politicians. In 1976 she was chosen to give the keynote address at the Democratic National Convention, making her both the first African American and the first woman to be selected as the keynote speaker for a major party convention. Speaking in support of the relatively unknown Jimmy Carter, she emphasized "unity, equality, accountability, and American ideals." Her eloquent and dramatic address has been called one of the most significant American political speeches of the twentieth century, and it was considered a major factor in securing the presidential nomination for Carter.

In the general election for president in November, Carter narrowly beat his Republican rival, President Gerald Ford, who was Nixon's successor. Upon taking office, President Carter offered Barbara several positions in his administration, but none was the one she wanted: attorney general. Rather than take a lesser cabinet position, she chose to remain in Congress.

Several years earlier, in 1973, Barbara had been diagnosed with multiple sclerosis, a progressive disease that would eventually take its toll on her ability to work. She served in Congress for as long as she could, bravely battling through pain and physical weakness for several years. She had planned to run for a seat in the U.S. Senate in 1978, but her MS had become worse, compelling her to retire from the strenuous demands of political life.

In 1979 Barbara published her autobiography, *Barbara Jordan: A Self Portrait*. Also that year, she accepted a teaching position at the University of Texas at Austin, which was, ironically, the same school she had not been allowed to attend as a young woman due to segregation. Her classes in political ethics and intergovernmental relations at the Lyndon Baines Johnson School of Public Affairs were so popular that enrollment was determined by lottery. Barbara taught at the School of Public Affairs until her death, serving for several of those years as the LBJ Centennial Chairman in National Policy.

Barbara's exit from electoral politics did not mean she no longer had influence in the political arena. In 1987 she spoke out strongly against Supreme Court nominee Robert Bork, who was nevertheless confirmed as a Supreme Court justice. Barbara served as an adviser to Texas governor Ann Richards in the early 1990s, and in 1992 she again gave the keynote address at the Democratic

National Convention. Appointed chairwoman of President Bill Clinton's Commission on Immigration Reform in 1994, she drew praise for her skillful management of that committee.

Over her lifetime, Barbara Jordan received innumerable honors and awards. In addition to her thirty-one honorary doctorate degrees, she received the NAACP (National Association for the Advancement of Colored People) Spingarn Medal in 1972; was named Best Living Orator in 1985; was inducted into the National Women's Hall of Fame in 1990; was the first recipient of the Nelson Mandela Award for Health and Human Rights in 1993; and was presented with the Presidential Medal of Freedom by President Bill Clinton in 1994. In the early 1990s, after popular Texas columnist Molly Ivins quipped that because of her resonant and commanding voice, Jordan would be the ideal choice to play the role of God Almighty in a Hollywood movie, the description "Voice of God" became permanently associated with Barbara's name, especially among her students.

Barbara never married. Her closest personal relationship was with her longtime companion Nancy Earl, with whom she lived for nearly thirty years, though neither Barbara nor Nancy ever confirmed that they had a romantic partnership. Nancy helped care for Barbara in her later years, when the multiple sclerosis confined her to a wheelchair. In spite of the MS, Barbara might have lived a longer life, but in 1994 she was diagnosed with leukemia as well.

Barbara Charline Jordan died on January 17, 1996, at age sixty, from complications of her leukemia. Her body lay in state at the LBJ Library at the University of Texas at Austin. She was interred in the State Cemetery in Austin, becoming the first black woman to be so honored. Her papers are housed at the Barbara Jordan Archives at Texas Southern University.

Many memorials to Barbara Jordan appeared after her death, and she continues to be honored to this day. Anyone arriving at the

Austin-Bergstrom International Airport will see a life-size bronze statue of Barbara in the ultramodern passenger terminal named for her; the terminal was built in 1999, and the statue was unveiled in 2002. A play about Barbara's life, *Voice of Good Hope*, premiered in Chicago in 2000, to much acclaim. In 2009 another bronze statue of the congresswoman, this one eight feet tall, was dedicated at the University of Texas at Austin. And in 2011, a postage stamp with Barbara's image was released as part of the U.S. Postal Service's Black Heritage Series.

Immediately following Barbara's death, tributes to her were presented in both houses of Congress. In her speech to the U.S. Senate, California Senator Barbara Boxer concluded:

> Throughout her life, Barbara Jordan was a voice for common ground, for the ties that bind. Hers were powerful, healing, uplifting words that challenged and inspired women and minorities, indeed all Americans, to reach for something higher and to believe in . . . their own ability to change the world and make it a better place. Her life was a testament to that idea.

Sources

FRANCITA ALAVEZ

Coalson, George O. "Alavez, Francita." In *Handbook of Texas Online.* http://www.tshaonline.org/handbook/online/articles/fal53 (accessed November 26, 2010).

Davenport, Harbert. "The Men of Goliad." *Southwestern Historical Quarterly*, July 1939.

Edwards, Janet R. "Remembering Goliad." *Texas Parks and Wildlife*, November 1992.

Hamilton, Lester D. *Goliad Survivor: Isaac D. Hamilton.* San Antonio: Naylor Company, 1971.

LaRoche, Clarence J. "Angel of Goliad Reputed First Nurse of America." Photocopy of article in unidentified newspaper, n.d. Archives, Daughters of the Republic of Texas Library, the Alamo, San Antonio, Texas.

O'Shea, Elena Zamora. "Legend of Angel of Goliad." Photocopy of article in unidentified newspaper, 1936. Archives, Daughters of the Republic of Texas Library, the Alamo, San Antonio, Texas.

Rogers, Marjorie. "Mystery of Angel of Goliad." Photocopy of article in unidentified newspaper, n.d. Archives, Daughters of the Republic of Texas Library, the Alamo, San Antonio, Texas.

Ruff, Ann. "Angel of Goliad." *Texas Highways*, August 1986.

Selden, Jack. "Remember Goliad." *Texas Highways*, October 1984.

Smith, Ruby Cumby. "James W. Fannin, Jr., in the Texas Revolution." *Southwestern Historical Quarterly,* October 1919.

Teer, L. P. "Angel of Goliad." *The West*, July 1965.

Thompson, Sam J. "Angel of Goliad." Photocopy of article in unidentified newspaper, n.d. Archives, Daughters of the Republic of Texas Library, the Alamo, San Antonio, Texas.

Tolbert, Frank X. "Tolbert's Texas." *Dallas News*, February 8, 1956.

Walraven, Bill. "Angel of Goliad Aided Many Texians." *Goliad Advance Guard*, March 22, 1990.

_____. "Not All Has Been Told about the Angel of Goliad." *Corpus Christi Caller Times*, October 10, 1986.

Wortham, Louis J. *A History of Texas*. Vol. 3. Fort Worth: Wortham-Molyneaux, 1924.

ELISABET NEY

Beazley, Julia. "Liendo Plantation." In *Handbook of Texas Online*. http://www.tshaonline.org/handbook/online/articles/ccl01 (accessed November 5, 2010).

Cutrer, Emily F. "Ney, Elisabet." In *Handbook of Texas Online*. http://www.tshaonline.org/handbook/online/articles/fne26 (accessed October 9, 2010).

Goar, Marjory. *Marble Dust: The Life of Elisabet Ney, An Interpretation*. Edited by Thomas Goar. Austin: Eakin Press, 1984.

Lone Star Junction. "Elisabet Ney (1833–1907)." http://www.lsjunction cp.com/people/ney.htm (accessed May 13, 2011).

Nye, Mary Elizabeth. "Elisabet Ney: Texas First Lady of Sculpture." In *Legendary Ladies of Texas*. Edited by Francis Edward Abernethy. Denton: University of North Texas Press, 1994.

Stephens, I. K. "Montgomery, Edmund Duncan." *Handbook of Texas Online*. http://www.tshaonline.org/handbook/online/articles/fmo10 (accessed May 13, 2011).

University of Texas at Austin. "Elisabet Ney: Sculptor, 1833–1907." *Great Texas Women*. http://www.utexas.edu./gtw/ney.php (accessed May 13, 2011).

ELIZABETH JOHNSON WILLIAMS

Branda, Eldon S. "Friday Mountain Ranch." In *The New Handbook of Texas*. Vol 3. Edited by Ron Tyler. Austin: Texas State Historical Association, 1996.

Crawford, Ann Fears, and Crystal Sasse Ragsdale. "A Texas Cattle Queen: Lizzie Johnson Williams." In *Women in Texas*. Austin: State House Press, 1992.

Duncan, Roberta S. "Elizabeth Ellen Johnson Williams." In *The New Handbook of Texas.* Vol 6. Edited by Ron Tyler. Austin: Texas State Historical Association, 1996.

Garrett, E. "Pioneer School Teacher Amassed a Fortune." *Frontier Times*, February 1928.

Myers, Cindi. "Taking Stock." *Texas Highways*, December 2001.

Peterson, John Allen. "William H. Day" *The New Handbook of Texas.* Vol 2. Edited by Ron Tyler. Austin: Texas State Historical Association, 1996.

Shelton, Emily Jones. "Lizzie E. Johnson: A Cattle Queen of Texas." *Southwestern Historical Quarterly*, January 1947.

Stovall, Frances, et al. *Clear Springs and Limestone Ledges: A History of San Marcos and Hays County.* Hays County, Texas: Hays County Historical Commission, 1986.

Taylor, T. U. "Johnson Institute." *Frontier Times*, February 1941.

Worcester, Donald E. "Chisholm Trail." In *The New Handbook of Texas.* Vol 2. Edited by Ron Tyler. Austin: Texas State Historical Association, 1996.

MOLLIE KIRKLAND BAILEY

Barton, Barbara. "Good Golly, Aunt Mollie." *Texas Highways*, April 2003.

Boulware, Narcissa Martin. "The Elephant in Montgomery . . ." (Part 5 of 5.) *Montgomery County News*, March 19, 2003. http://www.montgom erycountynews.net/archive01/ivebeenthink03-19-03.htm (accessed May 13, 2011).

___. "Following the Mollie Bailey Circus . . ." (Part 3 of 5.) *Montgomery County News*, March 5, 2003. http://www.montgomerycountynews .net/archive01/ivebeenthink03-05-03.htm (accessed May 13, 2011).

___. "Following the Mollie Bailey Circus . . ." (Part 4 of 5.) *Montgomery County News*, March 12, 2003. http://www.montgomerycountynews .net/archive01/ivebeenthink03-12-03.htm (accessed May 13, 2011).

___. "Mollie Bailey Brought the Circus to Montgomery." (Part 1 of 5.) *Montgomery County News*, February 19, 2003. http://www.montgom erycountynews.net/archive01/ivebeenthink02-19-03.htm (accessed May 13, 2011).

Boulware, Narcissa Martin. "Mollie Bailey Used Acting Talent . . ." (Part 2 of 5.) *Montgomery County News*, February 26, 2003. http://www.montgomerycountynews.net/archive01/ivebeenthink02-26-03.htm (accessed May 13, 2011).

Gurasich, Marj. *Red Wagons and White Canvas: A Story of the Mollie Bailey Circus.* Austin: Eakin Press, 1988.

Hartzog, Martha. "Mollie Bailey: Circus Entrepreneur." In *Legendary Ladies of Texas.* Edited by Francis Edward Abernethy. Denton: University of North Texas Press, 1994.

Heinonen, Bob. "Mollie Bailey." In Bob Heinonen's Heroes of History. http://www.texasheroes.net/MollieBailey.html. (accessed May 13, 2011).

Kleiner, Diana J. "Bailey, Mollie Arline Kirkland." In *Handbook of Texas Online.* http://www.tshaonline.org/handbook/online/articles/fba12 (accessed May 13, 2011).

Schwarz, Frederic. "Time Machine June/July." *American Heritage,* July 2006.

Troesser, John. "Mollie Bailey." http://www.texasescapes.com/They-Shoe-Horses-Dont-They/Mollie-Bailey.htm (accessed May 13, 2011).

World Book Encyclopedia. Chicago: World Book, 1987.

CLARA DRISCOLL

Ables, L. Robert. "Zavala, Adina Emilia De." In *Handbook of Texas Online.* http://www.tshaonline.org/handbook/online/articles/fzafg (accessed November 6, 2010).

"Clara Driscoll's Philanthropy to Crippled Children." Photocopy of article in unidentified newspaper, n.d. Archives, Daughters of the Republic of Texas Library, the Alamo, San Antonio, Texas.

Corpus Christi Caller. "Tribute Paid to Mrs. Clara Sevier Driscoll at Banquet." March 30, 1932.

DeMoss, Dorothy D. "Driscoll, Clara." In *Handbook of Texas Online.* http://www.tshaonline.org/handbook/online/articles/fdr04 (accessed November 5, 2010).

"Driscoll, Clara." File, n.d. Archives, Daughters of the Republic of Texas Library, the Alamo, San Antonio, Texas.

Long, Charles J. "The Alamo and Clara Driscoll." Press release, October 25, 1978. Archives, Daughters of the Republic of Texas Library, the Alamo, San Antonio, Texas.

Molyneaux, Peter. "How the Alamo Was Saved." *Bunker's Monthly*, 1928. Archives, Daughters of the Republic of Texas Library, the Alamo, San Antonio, Texas.

Pan American Round Tables of Texas (PARTT). Home page. http://partt .org/ (accessed May 13, 2011).

Quill, John. "Saving the Alamo." *The Texas Pioneer*, n.d. Archives, Daughters of the Republic of Texas Library, the Alamo, San Antonio, Texas.

Rash, Mrs. Grady, Jr. "Daughters of the Republic of Texas." In *Handbook of Texas Online*. http://www.tshaonline.org/handbook/online/articles/ vnd03 (accessed November 7, 2010).

Rogers, Mary Beth, Sherry A. Smith, and Janelle D. Scott. *We Can Fly*. Austin: Ellen C. Temple, Publisher, in cooperation with Texas Foundation for Women's Resources, 1983.

Turner, Martha Anne. "Clara Driscoll & Laguna Gloria History." In *Clara Driscoll: An American Tradition*. http://kaykeys.net/passions/ lagunagloria/history.html (accessed May 13, 2011).

Vela, Tammy. "Fiesta in San Antonio, Texas: Battle of Flowers Parade." http://www.essortment.com/fiesta-san-antonio-texas-battle-flowers -parade-32351.html (accessed May 13, 2011).

Walker, Horace C. "The Capitol of Texas." *Frontier Times*, May 1947.

MINNIE FISHER CUNNINGHAM

Campbell, Randolph B. *Gone to Texas: A History of the Lone Star State*. New York: Oxford University Press, 2003.

Cunningham, Patricia Ellen. "Cunningham, Minnie Fisher." In *Handbook of Texas Online*. http://tshaonlineorg/handbook/online/articles/ fcu24 (accessed November 24, 2010).

Eudy, John Carroll. "The Vote and Lone Star Women: Minnie Fisher Cunningham and the Texas Equal Suffrage Association." *East Texas Historical Journal* 14, Fall 1976.

Spencer, Cheryl. "Minnie Fisher Cunningham." From Newton Gresham Library, Sam Houston State University, *Musings from Sam Houston's Stomping Grounds* podcast series, episode 24, September 26, 2007. Adapted from the *Huntsville Item,* May 10, 1987. http://library.shsu .edu/about/podcasts/transcripts/Musings_Cunningham09262007.pdf.

JOVITA IDAR

Acosta, Teresa Palomo. "La Crónica." In *Handbook of Texas Online.* http://www.tshaonline.org/handbook/online/articles/eel06 (accessed November 11, 2010).

_____. "Idar, Nicasio." In *Handbook of Texas Online.* http://www.tsha online.org/handbook/online/articles/fid02 (accessed November 6, 2010).

Garza, Toni T. "Jovita Idar." http://www.myharlingennews.com/?p= 8572 (accessed May 13, 2011).

Jones, Nancy Baker. "Idar, Jovita." In *Handbook of Texas Online.* http://www.tshaonline.org/handbook/online/articles/fid03 (accessed October 9, 2010).

_____. "Villegas de Magnon, Leonor." In *Handbook of Texas Online.* http://www.tshaonline.org/handbook/online/articles/fvi19 (accessed November 6, 2010).

Koenig, Rebeca Anne Todd. "Rodriguez, Antonio." In *Handbook of Texas Online.* http://www.tshaonline.org/handbook/online/articles/fro99 (accessed November 9, 2010).

Leyva, Yolanda Chávez. "'*Por la raza y para la raza*': A Look at Tejana Activists, 1900–1998." http://utminers.utep.edu/yleyva/Tejana%20 Activists.htm (accessed May 13, 2011).

Lone Star Publishing. "Jovita Idar Juarez: Teacher, Journalist, Political Activist." In *Celebrating Texas: Lone Star Legends* (pdf). Austin: Lone Star Publishing J.V., 2003. http://www.celebratingtexas.com/tr/lsl/ lslFM.pdf (accessed May 13, 2011).

Morrell, Lea Anne. "Los Ojuelos, Texas." In *Handbook of Texas Online.* http://www.tshaonline.org/handbook/online/articles/hrl45 (accessed November 8, 2010).

Pisano, Marina. "Fierce Feminista." *San Antonio Express News*, October 2, 2001.

Rogers, Mary Beth, Sherry A. Smith, and Janelle D. Scott. *We Can Fly.* Austin: Ellen C. Temple, Publisher, in cooperation with Texas Foundation for Women's Resources, 1983.

BESSIE COLEMAN

Anderson, Greta. "Bessie Coleman (1893–1926): Flying for the Race." In *More Than Petticoats: Remarkable Texas Women*. Guilford, CT: Globe Pequot Press, 2002.

Answers.com. "Bessie Coleman, Aviator." http://www.answers.com/topic/bessie-coleman (accessed May 13, 2011).

Atlanta Historical Museum. "Bessie Coleman, 1892–1926." http://www.bessiecoleman.com/default.html (accessed May 13, 2011).

Eckerman, Jo. "Texas Women Take to the Air." Photocopy, 1986. Archives, Daughters of the Republic of Texas Library, the Alamo, San Antonio, Texas.

Karkabi, Barbara. "'Brave Bessie' Coleman Fought to Fly." *Houston Chronicle*, February 1996.

Morales, Roni. "Coleman, Bessie." In *Handbook of Texas Online*. http://www.tshaonline.org/handbook/online/articles/fcobq (accessed October 9, 2010).

Onkst, David H. "Bessie Coleman." http://www.centennialofflight.gov/essay/Explorers_Record_Setters_and_Daredevils/Coleman/EX11.htm (accessed May 13, 2011).

WGBH Educational Foundation. "Bessie Coleman (1892–1926)." In *Fly Girls*. Film for *The American Experience*. Silverlining Productions. http://www.pbs.org/wgbh/amex/flygirls/peopleevents/pandeAMEX02.html (accessed May 13, 2011).

White, Penny. "Bessie Coleman: First Black Aviator, Queen Bess Barnstormed into History." http://www.suite101.com/content/bessie-coleman-a146160?temp (accessed May 13, 2011).

Women in History. "Bessie Coleman." Lakewood Public Library. http://www.lkwdpl.org/wihohio/cole-bes.htm (accessed June 8, 2011).

OVETA CULP HOBBY

Answers.com. "Chautauqua." http://www.answers.com/topic/chautaupua-movement. (accessed May 13, 2011).

Answers.com. "Oveta Culp Hobby." http://www.answers.com/topic/oveta-culp-hobby (accessed May 13, 2011).

Chambers, John Whiteclay, II. *The Oxford Companion to American Military History*. 2000. http://www.encyclopedia.com/doc/10126-HobbyOvetaCulp.html (accessed May 13, 2011).

Findagrave.com. "Oveta Culp Hobby." http://www.findagrave.com/cgi
-bin/fg.cgi?page = gr&GRid = 19366 (accessed May 13, 2011).

Fondren Library, Rice University. "Oveta Culp Hobby and the Wom-
en's Army Corps Exhibit." http://library.rice.edu/collections/WRC/
digital-archive-information/online-exhilbits/oveta-culp-hobby-and
-the-women-s-army-corps-exhibit/?searchterm = oveta % 20culp % 20
hobby (accessed May 13, 2011).

Hobby, William, Jr. "Hobby, William Pettus." In *Handbook of Texas
Online.* http://www.tshaonline.org/handbook/online/articles/fho04
(accessed May 13, 2011).

National Women's Hall of Fame. "Oveta Culp Hobby." http://www.great
women.org/component/fabrik/details/2/75 (accessed May 13, 2011).

Time Magazine. "The Cabinet: Lady in Command." May 4, 1953. http://
www.time.com/time/magazine/article/0,9171,818360-1,00.html
(accessed May 13, 2011).

Tyler, Ron, ed. "Hobby, Oveta Culp." In *The New Handbook of Texas.* Austin: Texas State Historical Association, 1996.

Wikipedia.org. "Federal Security Agency." http://en.wikipedia.org/wiki/
Federal_Security_Agency (accessed May 13, 2011).

BABE DIDRIKSON ZAHARIAS

Answers.com. "Babe Didrikson Zaharias." http://www.answers.com/
topic/babe-didrikson-zaharias (accessed May 13, 2011).

Caylef, Susan E. "Zaharias, Mildred Ella Didrikson [Babe]." In *Handbook of Texas Online.* http://www.tshaonline.org/handbook/online/
articles/fza01 (accessed May 13, 2011).

Johnson, William Oscar, and Nancy P. Williamson. *Whatta Gal: The Babe
Didrikson Story.* Boston: Little, Brown & Company, 1975.

Knief, Mary Kay. "The Babe." In *Legendary Ladies of Texas.* Edited by
Francis Edward Abernethy. Denton: University of North Texas Press,
1994.

National Women's Hall of Fame. "Mildred 'Babe' Didrikson Zaharias."
http://www.greatwomen.org/women-of-the-hall/search-the-hall/
details/2/176-Zaharias (accessed May 13, 2011).

Publications International. "Babe Didrikson Zaharias." http://enter
tainment.howstuffworks.com/babe-didrikson-zaharias-golfer.htm
(accessed May 13, 2011).

Rogers, Mary Beth, Sherry A. Smith, and Janelle D. Scott. *We Can Fly.*
Austin: Ellen C. Temple, publisher, in cooperation with Texas Foundation for Women's Resources, 1983.

Who2.com. "Babe Didrikson Zaharias Biography." http://www.who2
.com/babedidriksonzaharias.html (accessed May 13, 2011).

Wikipedia.org. "George Zaharias." http://www.en.wikipedia.org/wiki/
George_Zaharias (accessed May 13, 2011).

BARBARA JORDAN

Answers.com. "Barbara Jordan." answers.com/topic/barbara-jordan
(accessed December 19, 2010).

Barkley, Roy R., and Mark F. Odintz, eds. *The Portable Handbook of Texas.*
Austin: Texas State Historical Association, 2000.

Butler, Bonita Jackson. "Barbara Jordan, 1936–1996." beejae.com/bjor
dan.htm (accessed December 15, 2010).

Campbell, Randolph B. *Gone To Texas: A History of the Lone Star State.*
New York: Oxford University Press, 2003.

Kleiner, Diana J. "Fifth Ward Houston." In *Handbook of Texas Online.*
http://tshaonline.org/handbook/online/articles/hpfhk (accessed
December 13, 2010).

Odintz, Mark. "Jordan, Barbara Charline." In *Handbook of Texas Online.*
http://tshaonline.org/handbook/online/articles/fjoas (accessed
December 15, 2010).

Wikipedia.org. "Texas Southern University." http://en.wikipedia.org/
wiki/Texas_Southern_University (accessed December 16, 2010).

Index

Photographs appear in italics

DON BLEVINS, a native of Tennessee, retired from the U.S. Air Force in 1972 after twenty-one years of service and moved to San Marcos, Texas, where he took up a pen. His articles have been published in more than fifty regional, travel, and special-interest periodicals, and he is the author of five previous books: *Texas: Mapping the Lone Star State Through History* (Globe Pequot Press, 2010); *A Priest, a Prostitute, and Some Other Early Texans: The Lives of Fourteen Lone Star State Pioneers* (Two Dot, 2008); *Texas Towns: From Abner to Zipperlandville* (Republic of Texas Press, 2003); *From Angels to Hellcats: Legendary Texas Women, 1836 to 1880* (Mountain Press Publishing, 2001); and *Peculiar, Uncertain, and Two Egg: The Unusual Origins of More Than 3,000 American Place Names* (Cumberland House Publishing, 2000).